# TEACHER'S PET PUBLICATIONS

## LITPLAN TEACHER PACK
for
The Scarlet Letter
based on the book by
Nathaniel Hawthorne

Written by
Mary B. Collins

© 1997 Teacher's Pet Publications
All Rights Reserved

This **Lit Plan** for Nathaniel Hawthorne's
*The Scarlet Letter*
has been brought to you by Teacher's Pet Publications, Inc.

Copyright Teacher's Pet Publications 1997
11504 Hammock Point
Berlin MD 21811

Only the student materials in this unit plan
such as worksheets, study questions, assignment sheets, and tests
may be reproduced multiple times for use in the purchaser's classroom.

For any additional copyright questions,
contact Teacher's Pet Publications.

www.tpet.com

# TABLE OF CONTENTS - *The Scarlet Letter*

| | |
|---|---|
| Introduction | 5 |
| Unit Objectives | 8 |
| Reading Assignment Sheet | 9 |
| Unit Outline | 10 |
| Study Questions (Short Answer) | 13 |
| Quiz/Study Questions (Multiple Choice) | 19 |
| Pre-reading Vocabulary Worksheets | 29 |
| Lesson One (Introductory Lesson) | 47 |
| Nonfiction Assignment Sheet | 49 |
| Oral Reading Evaluation Form | 51 |
| Writing Assignment 1 | 53 |
| Writing Assignment 2 | 66 |
| Writing Assignment 3 | 72 |
| Writing Evaluation Form | 55 |
| Vocabulary Review Activities | 57 |
| Extra Writing Assignments/Discussion ?s | 59 |
| Unit Review Activities | 74 |
| Unit Tests | 77 |
| Unit Resource Materials | 107 |
| Vocabulary Resource Materials | 121 |

# A FEW NOTES ABOUT THE AUTHOR
# NATHANIEL HAWTHORNE

HAWTHORNE, Nathaniel (1804-64). Although his friends and acquaintances included a number of noted transcendental thinkers and writers-such as Ralph Waldo Emerson, Henry David Thoreau, and Bronson Alcott-Nathaniel Hawthorne's works show little of the optimism and self-confidence that marked transcendental philosophy. Instead, he preferred themes drawn more from a Puritan preoccupation with guilt and the natural depravity of humans.

Hawthorne was born on July 4, 1804, in Salem, Mass. His family, early Puritan settlers in America, had lived in Salem since the 1600s. One of his ancestors may have been a judge in the Salem witchcraft trials. Hawthorne's father, a ship's captain, died when Nathaniel was only 4, and his mother became a virtual recluse. Hawthorne attended Bowdoin College in Brunswick, Me., where he befriended Franklin Pierce, who later became a president of the United States.

Hawthorne decided to become a writer, but until the 1840s he wrote little except for an amateurish novel, 'Fanshawe', published anonymously at his own expense in 1828. Some stories he sold to magazines were published as 'Twice Told Tales' in 1837. The publication cost of the collection was underwritten by another of his college friends, Horatio Bridge. He worked in the Boston Customhouse from 1839 to 1840, after which he spent a few months at Brook Farm, a cooperative agricultural community in West Roxbury, Mass. The Brook Farm experience was later described in 'The Blithedale Romance' (1852).

In 1842 Hawthorne married Sophia Peabody. The young couple spent the next three years in the Old Manse in Concord, where he wrote a second series of 'Twice Told Tales'. 'Mosses from an Old Manse', published in 1846, describes their happy life in Concord. In 1845 Hawthorne returned to Salem and again worked in a customhouse. Relieved of that job in 1849, he found time to write. His best-known work, 'The Scarlet Letter', was published in 1850. Moving from Salem to Lenox, Mass., Hawthorne wrote 'The House of the Seven Gables', which came out the following year. At Lenox he made the acquaintance of Herman Melville, a fellow writer whose novels show Hawthorne's influence. After a short stay in West Newton, Mass., the Hawthornes returned to Concord, where they purchased a house that had belonged to Bronson Alcott, renaming it Wayside.

In 1853 Franklin Pierce became president. He offered Hawthorne a consulship in Liverpool, England, a post that Hawthorne held until 1857. After resigning his position as consul, Hawthorne traveled in Europe, mostly in Italy. In 1860 the Hawthornes returned to their home in Concord. After 'The Marble Faun', published that year, Hawthorne wrote little. He aged rapidly and found it increasingly difficult to write. On May 19, 1864, while traveling with his friend Pierce, Hawthorne died in Plymouth, N.H.

--- Courtesy of Compton's Learning Company

# INTRODUCTION - *The Scarlet Letter*

This unit has been designed to develop students' reading, writing, thinking, and language skills through exercises and activities related to *The Scarlet Letter* by Nathaniel Hawthorne. It includes eighteen lessons, supported by extra resource materials.

The **introductory lesson** introduces students to one main theme of the novel through a group activity. Following the introductory activity, students are given a transition to explain how the activity relates to the book they are about to read. Following the transition, students are given the materials they will be using during the unit. At the end of the lesson, students begin the pre-reading work for the first reading assignment.

The **reading assignments** are approximately thirty pages each; some are a little shorter while others are a little longer. Students have approximately 15 minutes of pre-reading work to do prior to each reading assignment. This pre-reading work involves reviewing the study questions for the assignment and doing some vocabulary work for 8 to 10 vocabulary words they will encounter in their reading.

The **study guide questions** are fact-based questions; students can find the answers to these questions right in the text. These questions come in two formats: short answer or multiple choice. The best use of these materials is probably to use the short answer version of the questions as study guides for students (since answers will be more complete), and to use the multiple choice version for occasional quizzes. If your school has the appropriate machinery, it might be a good idea to make transparencies of your answer keys for the overhead projector.

The **vocabulary work** is intended to enrich students' vocabularies as well as to aid in the students' understanding of the book. Prior to each reading assignment, students will complete a two-part worksheet for approximately 8 to 10 vocabulary words in the upcoming reading assignment. Part I focuses on students' use of general knowledge and contextual clues by giving the sentence in which the word appears in the text. Students are then to write down what they think the words mean based on the words' usage. Part II nails down the definitions of the words by giving students dictionary definitions of the words and having students match the words to the correct definitions based on the words' contextual usage. Students should then have a good understanding of the words when they meet them in the text.

After each reading assignment, students will go back and formulate answers for the study guide questions. Discussion of these questions serves as a **review** of the most important events and ideas presented in the reading assignments.

After students complete reading the work, there is a **vocabulary review** lesson which pulls together all of the fragmented vocabulary lists for the reading assignments and gives students a review of all of the words they have studied.

Following the vocabulary review, a lesson is devoted to the **extra discussion questions/writing assignments**. These questions focus on interpretation, critical analysis and personal response, employing a variety of thinking skills and adding to the students' understanding of the novel.

The **group activity** which follows the discussion questions has students working in small groups to discuss symbolism in the novel. Using the information they have acquired so far through individual work and class discussions, students get together to further examine the text and to brainstorm ideas relating to the symbols used in the novel. The group activity is followed by a **reports and discussion** session in which the groups share their ideas about the symbols with the entire class so the entire class can discuss symbolism in *The Scarlet Letter* based on the nucleus of information brought forth by each of the groups.

There are three **writing assignments** in this unit, each with the purpose of informing, persuading, or having students express personal opinions. The first assignment is to persuade: students write a letter to Governor Bellingham persuading him to do what they think should be done about Hester and Pearl. The second assignment is to inform: following the reports and discussion, students write a composition in which they explain symbolism in the book, based on the information given in class and the students' own personal reflections. In the third writing assignment, students express their own opinions about what it would be like to be in jail.

In addition, there is a **nonfiction reading assignment**. Students are required to read a piece of nonfiction related in some way to *The Scarlet Letter* (articles about prejudice or coming of age, trial transcripts, etc.). After reading their nonfiction pieces, students will fill out a worksheet on which they answer questions regarding facts, interpretation, criticism, and personal opinions. During one class period, students make **oral presentations** about the nonfiction pieces they have read. This not only exposes all students to a wealth of information, it also gives students the opportunity to practice **public speaking**.

The **review lesson** pulls together all of the aspects of the unit. The teacher is given four or five choices of activities or games to use which all serve the same basic function of reviewing all of the information presented in the unit.

The **unit test** comes in two formats: all multiple choice-matching-true/false or with a mixture of matching, short answer, multiple choice, and composition. As a convenience, two different tests for each format have been included.

There are additional **support materials** included with this unit. The **extra activities packet** includes suggestions for an in-class library, crossword and word search puzzles related to the novel, and extra vocabulary worksheets. There is a list of **bulletin board ideas** which gives the teacher suggestions for bulletin boards to go along with this unit. In addition, there is a list of **extra class activities** the teacher could choose from to enhance the unit or as a substitution for an exercise the teacher might feel is inappropriate for his/her class. **Answer keys** immediately follow the **reproducible student materials** in the unit. Student materials may be reproduced for use in the teacher's classroom without infringement of copyrights. No other part of the unit may be reproduced without the written consent of Teacher's Pet Publications, Inc.

The **level** of this unit can be varied depending upon the criteria on which the individual assignments are graded, the teacher's expectations of his/her students in class discussions, and the formats chosen for the study guides, quizzes and test. If teachers have other ideas/activities they wish to use, they can usually easily be inserted prior to the review lesson.

# UNIT OBJECTIVES - *The Scarlet Letter*

1. While reading Hawthorne's *The Scarlet Letter* students will consider the issues of crime and punishment, morality vs. legality, and personal responsibility.

2. Students will demonstrate their understanding of the text on four levels: factual, interpretive, critical and personal.

3. Students will define their own viewpoints on the aforementioned themes.

4. Students will gain a better understanding of Puritan theocracy and its effects on ordinary citizens.

5. Students will study the use of symbolism in *The Scarlet Letter*.

6. Students will be given the opportunity to practice reading aloud and silently to improve their skills in each area.

7. Students will answer questions to demonstrate their knowledge and understanding of the main events and characters in *The Scarlet Letter* as they relate to the author's theme development.

8. Students will enrich their vocabularies and improve their understanding of the novel through the vocabulary lessons prepared for use in conjunction with the novel.

9. The writing assignments in this unit are geared to several purposes:
    a. To have students demonstrate their abilities to inform, to persuade, or to express their own personal ideas
        Note: Students will demonstrate ability to write effectively to <u>inform</u> by developing and organizing facts to convey information. Students will demonstrate the ability to write effectively to <u>persuade</u> by selecting and organizing relevant information, establishing an argumentative purpose, and by designing an appropriate strategy for an identified audience. Students will demonstrate the ability to write effectively to <u>express personal ideas</u> by selecting a form and its appropriate elements.
    b. To check the students' reading comprehension
    c. To make students think about the ideas presented by the novel
    d. To encourage logical thinking
    e. To provide an opportunity to practice good grammar and improve students' use of the English language.

10. Students will read aloud, report, and participate in large and small group discussions to improve their public speaking and personal interaction skills.

# READING ASSIGNMENT SHEET - *The Scarlet Letter*

| Date Assigned | Reading Assignment (Chapters) | Completion Date |
|---|---|---|
|  | 1-4 |  |
|  | 5-7 |  |
|  | 8-10 |  |
|  | 11-13 |  |
|  | 14-17 |  |
|  | 18-21 |  |
|  | 22-24 |  |

## UNIT OUTLINE - *The Scarlet Letter*

| 1<br>Introduction | 2<br>PVR 1-4 | 3<br>Study ?s 1-4<br><br>PVR 5-7 | 4<br>Study ?s 5-7<br>Writing Assignment 1<br>PV 8-10 | 5<br>Read 8-10<br><br>PVR 11-13 |
|---|---|---|---|---|
| 6<br>Study ?s 8-13<br>Writing Conf. Working Time<br>PVR 14-17 | 7<br>Study ?s 14-17<br><br>PVR 18-21 | 8<br>Study ?s 18-21<br><br>PVR 22-24 | 9<br>Study ?s 22-24<br><br>Vocabulary | 10<br>Library<br><br>Assign Discussion ?s |
| 11<br><br>Discussion | 12<br><br>Group Activity | 13<br><br>Writing Assignment 2 | 14<br><br>Game | 15<br><br>Nonfiction Discussion |
| 16<br>Activity: Crime And Punishment | 17<br>Writing Assignment 3 | 18<br>Review | 19<br>Test | |

Key:  P = Preview Study Questions   V = Vocabulary Work   R = Read

# STUDY GUIDE QUESTIONS

# SHORT ANSWER STUDY GUIDE QUESTIONS - *The Scarlet Letter*

## Chapters 1-4
1. Identify Hester Prynne, Pearl, Rev. Mr. Dimmesdale and Roger Chillingworth.
2. What emblem did Hester have to wear? Why was she sentenced to wear it?
3. What information did Hester refuse to tell the officials and Mr. Dimmesdale?
4. What was the relationship between Hester and Roger Chillingworth?
5. What did Hester promise to Roger Chillingworth?

## Chapters 5-7
1. Hester is released from prison. Why doesn't she run away to a different settlement?
2. How did Hester support herself and Pearl?
3. Describe Pearl.
4. Describe Hester's feelings towards Pearl.
5. Why did Hester go to see Governor Bellingham?
6. What did Hester and Pearl see in the breastplate of the armor? What is the significance of the exaggeration?

## Chapters 8-10
1. Mr. Wilson asks Pearl, "Canst thou tell me, my child, who made thee?" What is Pearl's answer? Why did she say that?
2. What convinced the Governor to let Hester keep Pearl?
3. How did Roger Chillingworth become Dimmesdale's medical advisor?
4. Who is the leech? Why is he called that in the title of the chapter?
5. Why did Mr. Dimmesdale rush from the room to end the conversation he had with Roger Chillingworth?

## Chapters 11-13
1. What does Rev. Dimmesdale's congregation think of him? Why is that ironic?
2. Where did Mr. Dimmesdale go at midnight? Why?
3. What did Pearl ask Mr. Dimmesdale?
4. What "sign" did the meteor make in the sky?
5. Where had Mr. Wilson, Hester, Pearl and Roger Chillingworth been that night, that they would all be walking by the scaffolding at midnight?
6. What was the other view of Hester?

## Chapters 14-17
1. What did Hester tell Roger Chillingworth when they met on the peninsula?
2. Why do Hester and Pearl go to the forest?
3. When Mr. Dimmesdale finds out that Roger Chillingworth is out for revenge, he knows his religious career in Boston will be at an end and his life will be miserable. What does Hester suggest?

Short Answer Study Questions *Scarlet Letter* page 2

Chapters 18-21
1. What did Hester have to do by the brook before Pearl would come across?
2. Mr. Dimmesdale kissed Pearl. What did she do in response?
3. How did Rev. Mr. Dimmesdale's attitude change after he decided to leave Boston with Hester?


Chapters 22-24
1. What shocking news did the commander of the Bristol ship bring Hester?
2. What did Mr. Dimmesdale tell the people of New England before he died?
3. What did the people see when Mr. Dimmesdale took off his ministerial band?
4. What happens to Hester, Pearl and Roger Chillingworth?

# ANSWER KEY: STUDY GUIDE QUESTIONS - *The Scarlet Letter*

Chapters 1-4
1. Identify Hester Prynne, Pearl, Rev. Mr. Dimmesdale and Roger Chillingworth.
    Hester Prynne is the main character of the novel. She is the one who has sinned and must wear a letter "A." The Rev. Mr. Dimmesdale talks to Hester on the scaffolding, asking her to reveal the name of the man who sinned with her. In this first section, he appears overly earnest in his questioning of Hester. We later find out that he is, in fact, the other sinner. Roger Chillingworth is Hester's former husband. He remains in Boston under this assumed name and practices medicine. Pearl is Hester's daughter, a result of her affair with Dimmesdale.

2. What emblem did Hester have to wear? Why was she sentenced to wear it?
    Hester had to wear the letter "A" to show that she is guilty of adultery.

3. What information did Hester refuse to tell the officials and Mr. Dimmesdale?
    Hester refused to name the man who sinned with her.

4. What was the relationship between Hester and Roger Chillingworth?
    Hester had married Roger Prynne prior to coming to America. He loved her, but she didn't love him. It was a marriage they both hoped would work out, but she was never satisfied with the relationship. They were separated on the way to the colony, and when he didn't show up for a year, she assumed he was dead. He appeared in Boston on the day of her public punishment and assumed the name Chillingworth.

5. What did Hester promise to Roger Chillingworth?
    Hester promised not to reveal Roger's true identity.

Chapters 5-7
1. Hester is released from prison. Why doesn't she run away to a different settlement?
    "Here . . . had been the scene of her guilt, and here should be the scene of her earthly punishment; and so, perchance, the torture of her daily shame would at length purge her soul."

2. How did Hester support herself and Pearl?
    Hester did needlework.

3. Describe Pearl.
    Pearl was a physically beautiful child. Hester could "recognize her wild, desperate, defiant mood, the flightiness of her temper, and even some of the . . . gloom and despondency that brooded in her heart."

4. Describe Hester's feelings towards Pearl.
>Hester loved Pearl very much. She was always a little worried that, being the product of a sin, the child would exhibit some odd characteristics showing her as a child of the devil.

5. Why did Hester go to see Governor Bellingham?
>Hester went to see the governor because she had heard some people saying she should not have custody of Pearl. She wanted to talk to the governor to get him to let her keep the child.

6. What did Hester and Pearl see in the breastplate of the armor? What is the significance of the exaggeration?
>They see an enlarged, distorted letter "A" which symbolically shows the tremendous burden of Hester's sin. When people see her, they perhaps see her as she saw herself in the armor.

## Chapters 8-10

1. Mr. Wilson asks Pearl, "Canst thou tell me, my child, who made thee?" What is Pearl's answer? Why did she say that?
>She replies that she was plucked from the rose bush. She knew the correct answer but felt contrary.

2. What convinced the Governor to let Hester keep Pearl?
>Both Hester and Mr. Dimmesdale told the governor that Pearl was a constant reminder to Hester of her sin and that Hester was capable of being a good mother since she could pass along to Pearl the lessons she had learned since she had sinned.

3. How did Roger Chillingworth become Dimmesdale's medical advisor?
>The elder ministers of Boston and the deacons of the church "dealt with him" about the sin of rejecting medical help, so he saw Roger Chillingworth.

4. Who is the leech? Why is he called that in the title of the chapter?
>Roger Chillingworth is the leech. He is called that because he has latched on to Mr. Dimmesdale and is systematically not only sucking out information but also the life of Mr. Dimmesdale under the guise of being a helpful doctor.

5. Why did Mr. Dimmesdale rush from the room to end the conversation he had with Roger Chillingworth?
>Chillingworth suggested that Mr. Dimmesdale's illness was not just physical but rooted in some secret Mr. Dimmesdale held in his soul. Dimmesdale, recognizing Chillingworth's accuracy, does not wish to reveal his sin to anyone. He runs out of the room to avoid being trapped into a confession.

Chapters 11-13

1. What does Rev. Dimmesdale's congregation think of him? Why is that ironic?
    The congregation thinks Dimmesdale is practically a saint. The worse he feels about his sin and the harder he tries to confess and bring it into the open, the more saintly he becomes in the eyes of the people.

2. Where did Mr. Dimmesdale go at midnight? Why?
    He went to the public scaffolding where Hester had stood because he had some peculiar idea that standing there through the nights would in some way help him with his penance.

3. What did Pearl ask Mr. Dimmesdale?
    Pearl asked Dimmesdale if he would stand on the scaffolding, hand in hand, with Hester and her at noontime the next day.

4. What "sign" did the meteor make in the sky?
    It made a large letter A which glowed red.

5. Where had Mr. Wilson, Hester, Pearl and Roger Chillingworth been that night, that they would all be walking by the scaffolding at midnight?
    They had all been at the deathbed of Governor Winthrop.

6. What was the other view of Hester?
    Hester had taken to doing good works, living a simple, pure life. The people of Boston were beginning to recognize her as a person instead of just a sinner. Some even were beginning to say the "A" was for "Able."

Chapters 14-17

1. What did Hester tell Roger Chillingworth when they met on the peninsula?
    She told him that she would break her promise and identify him as her former husband.

2. Why do Hester and Pearl go to the forest?
    They go to the forest to intercept Dimmesdale on his journey home to Boston, to tell him that Chillingworth was really Hester's husband who was seeking revenge.

3. When Mr. Dimmesdale finds out that Roger Chillingworth is out for revenge, he knows his religious career in Boston will be at an end and his life will be miserable. What does Hester suggest?
    She suggests that Dimmesdale could move and leave his troubles behind. She also volunteers to go with him.

Chapters 18-21

1. What did Hester have to do by the brook before Pearl would come across?
    She had to put her letter A back on and pin her hair back up.

2. Mr. Dimmesdale kissed Pearl. What did she do in response?
   She ran to the brook and washed it off.

3. How did Rev. Mr. Dimmesdale's attitude change after he decided to leave Boston with Hester?
   He felt better and had more energy. He also has a real temptation to do some very bad things like "uttering certain blasphemous suggestions . . . regarding the communion supper" or teaching some wicked words to Puritan children.

Chapters 22-24
1. What shocking news did the commander of the Bristol ship bring Hester?
   She learned that Chillingworth had also booked passage on the ship.

2. What did Mr. Dimmesdale tell the people of New England before he died?
   He confessed that he was the one who had sinned with Hester, that Pearl was his child.

3. What did the people see when Mr. Dimmesdale took off his ministerial band?
   Some say they saw a scarlet letter.

4. What happens to Hester, Pearl and Roger Chillingworth?
   Chillingworth died within a year, leaving his property to Pearl, who we are led to believe married and lived on that property in England. Hester vanished with Pearl, but later she supposedly returned to Boston to finish her penance sentence there. She supposedly died there years later and was buried, we assume next to Dimmesdale.

# MULTIPLE CHOICE STUDY GUIDE/QUIZ QUESTIONS - *The Scarlet Letter*

<u>Chapters 1-4</u>

1. Identify:  A=Hester Prynne   B=Pearl   C=Rev. Mr. Dimmesdale   D=Roger Chillingworth

___ She has sinned and must wear the letter "A."

___ He asks the sinner to reveal the name of the man who sinned with her.

___ He is the sinner's former husband.

___ She is the daughter of the sinner.


2. For what did the letter A stand?
    a. Alone
    b. Adultery
    c. Adopted
    d. Aspersion

3. What information did Hester refuse to tell the officials and Mr. Dimmesdale?
    a. Against whom she had committed libel
    b. Where her former husband had gone
    c. The name of the man who had sinned with her
    d. The age of her daughter

4. What was the relationship between Hester and Roger Chillingworth?
    a. They were divorced.
    b. They were just married.
    c. They were married but had been separated.
    d. They were in love.

5. What did Hester promise to Roger Chillingworth?
    a. To conceal his true identity
    b. To give him the divorce he asked for
    c. Not to tell Rev. Dimmesdale about his sins
    d. Not to ever leave him again

*Scarlet Letter* Study/Quiz Questions Multiple Choice Format Page 2

Chapters 5-7

1. Hester is released from prison. Why doesn't she run away to a different settlement?
	a. She is not allowed to under the terms of her release.
	b. She loves Rev. Dimmesdale and must remain near him.
	c. Pearl is too young to travel.
	d. She feels her soul may be purged clean if she remains living there, disgraced.

2. How did Hester support herself and Pearl?
	a. Sewing
	b. Growing & selling food
	c. Selling prayer books
	d. She couldn't support them; they depended on charity.

3. Describe Pearl.
	a. Beautiful but not smart
	b. Ugly and nasty
	c. Beautiful but unusual
	d. Not beautiful, but sweet and docile

4. Describe Hester's feelings towards Pearl.
	a. She resented Pearl.
	b. She loved Pearl.
	c. She had no feelings one way or the other.
	d. She didn't even like Pearl.

5. Why did Hester go to see Governor Bellingham?
	a. To plead for her life
	b. To tell him Roger's true identity
	c. To plead to keep Pearl
	d. To tell him that Rev. Dimmesdale was the other sinner

6. What did Hester and Pearl see in the breastplate of the armor?
	a. A grotesque devil
	b. A crucifix
	c. Hester's "A"
	d. A reflection of the Bible

*Scarlet Letter* Study/Quiz Questions Multiple Choice Format Page 3

Chapters 8-10

1. Mr. Wilson asks Pearl, "Canst thou tell me, my child, who made thee?" What is Pearl's answer?
    a. "The Holy Father, God Almighty!"
    b. "I am a child of the devil's work."
    c. "I was plucked from the wild rose bush by my mother's prison door."
    d. "I don't know who made me."

2. What convinced the Governor to let Hester keep Pearl?
    a. Hester would constantly remind Pearl of the consequences of sin.
    b. Rev. Dimmesdale promised to watch the mother and child closely & report anything that might interest the governor
    c. Hester agreed to allow Chillingworth live with her and Pearl, so they could all be a "real family."
    d. It was just a whim, as was his customary way of making decisions.

3. How did Roger Chillingworth become Dimmesdale's medical advisor?
    a. Chillingworth paid him to be his first patient so he could get his medical practice started.
    b. The church elders and deacons reminded him it would be a sin not to seek medical help.
    c. Hester Prynne arranged it.
    d. Dimmesdale did it for Hester's sake.

4. Who is the leech?
    a. Dimmesdale
    b. Hester
    c. Pearl
    d. Chillingworth

5. Why did Mr. Dimmesdale rush from the room to end the conversation he had with Roger Chillingworth?
    a. To tend to an urgent call
    b. To make Chillingworth angry
    c. To keep from hitting Chillingworth
    d. To keep from being trapped into a confession

*Scarlet Letter* Study/Quiz Questions Multiple Choice Format Page 4

Chapters 11-13

1. What does Rev. Dimmesdale's congregation think of him?
    a. They think he's a pitiful minister.
    b. They think he's practically a saint.
    c. They think he's a horrible sinner.
    d. They think he's a weak man who succumbed to the temptations of life.

2. Where did Mr. Dimmesdale go at midnight?
    a. To the forest
    b. To Hester's house
    c. To the scaffolding
    d. To see Chillingworth

3. What did Pearl ask Mr. Dimmesdale?
    a. If he was her father
    b. If he was a brother to the devil
    c. If he would stand hand in hand with her & Hester on the scaffolding
    d. If he would help her mother make a better life for them

4. What "sign" did the meteor make in the sky?
    a. A crucifix
    b. An A
    c. A frown
    d. A pitchfork

5. Where had Mr. Wilson, Hester, Pearl and Roger Chillingworth been that night, that they would all be walking by the scaffolding at midnight?
    a. In the forest
    b. At the church
    c. At the governor's deathbed
    d. At Dimmesdale's special meeting

6. What were people beginning to think of Hester?
    a. They were beginning to think she was a witch as well as a sinner.
    b. They were beginning to recognize her as a person instead of as just a sinner.
    c. They were beginning to think she was "born bad."
    d. They were beginning to suspect that she had had an affair with Rev. Dimmesdale.

*Scarlet Letter* Study/Quiz Questions Multiple Choice Format Page 5

Chapters 14-17

1. What did Hester tell Roger Chillingworth when they met on the peninsula?
    a. Rev. Dimmesdale was sicker than even Chillingworth thought.
    b. She wanted Chillingworth to admit to being the "other sinner."
    c. She was going to break her promise to him.
    d. She couldn't help falling in love with him again.

2. Why do Hester and Pearl go to the forest?
    a. To enjoy nature's solitude
    b. To pick flowers
    c. To pray
    d. To intercept Dimmesdale

3. When Mr. Dimmesdale finds out that Roger Chillingworth is out for revenge, he knows his religious career in Boston will be at an end and his life will be miserable. What does Hester suggest?
    a. She suggests a plot to get rid of Chillingworth.
    b. She suggests that Dimmesdale should take Pearl and go away.
    c. She suggests that Dimmesdale should go away, taking her and Pearl, too.
    d. She suggests that Dimmesdale should stay and face his punishment as she has done, that, in doing so, his soul might also be cleansed before his life ends.

*Scarlet Letter* Study/Quiz Questions Multiple Choice Format Page 6

Chapters 18-21

1. What did Hester have to do by the brook before Pearl would come across?
    a. Make Dimmesdale go away
    b. Pin her A back on
    c. Promise to come to the brook again
    d. Promise that they would move away together

2. Mr. Dimmesdale kissed Pearl. What did she do in response?
    a. Ran to the brook and washed it off
    b. Spit at him
    c. Slapped him
    d. Hugged him

3. How did Rev. Mr. Dimmesdale's attitude change after he decided to leave Boston with Hester?
    a. Felt better
    b. Had more energy
    c. Felt temptation to do bad things
    d. All of the above

*Scarlet Letter* Study/Quiz Questions Multiple Choice Format Page 7

Chapters 22-24

1. What news did the commander of the Bristol ship bring Hester?
   a. The ship's departure would be delayed by at least three weeks.
   b. Chillingworth had taken Pearl on board the ship *Venturer*.
   c. Dimmesdale had already left on board the ship *Venturer*.
   d. Chillingworth had booked passage on the Bristol ship.

2. What did Mr. Dimmesdale tell the people of New England before he died?
   a. He confessed that he was the one who had sinned with Hester, that Pearl was his child.
   b. He told them to beware, to be watchful of their own souls; even the most pious among them is easy prey to temptation.
   c. He asked their eternal forgiveness and their pity upon Hester and Pearl.
   d. All of the above

3. What did the people see when Mr. Dimmesdale took off his ministerial band?
   a. Nothing; whatever he thought was there did not exist
   b. A grotesque image of the devil
   c. An imprint matching Hester's "A"
   d. The Eye of God

4. What happened to Hester?
   a. She vanished, never to be seen again.
   b. She vanished, but later returned to her home in Boston.
   c. She lived in her home in Boston for the rest of her days.
   d. She moved to a different settlement.

5. What happened to Chillingworth?
   a. He vanished.
   b. He gave up the practice of medicine to become a clergyman after seeing the error of his ways.
   c. He died within a year, leaving his property to Pearl.
   d. He died within a year, penniless, a broken, miserable man.

6. What happened to Pearl?
   a. She married and lived in her mother's home in Boston.
   b. She married and lived in England.
   c. She vanished, never to be heard of again.
   d. She moved to England to live as a recluse as penance for her mother's sins.

ANSWER KEY - MULTIPLE CHOICE STUDY/QUIZ QUESTIONS

| Chapters 1-4 | Chapters 5-7 | Chapters 8-10 | Chapters 11-13 |
|---|---|---|---|
| 1. A,C,D,B | 1. D | 1. C | 1. B |
| 2. B | 2. A | 2. A | 2. C |
| 3. C | 3. C | 3. B | 3. C |
| 4. C | 4. B | 4. D | 4. B |
| 5. A | 5. C | 5. D | 5. C |
|  | 6. C |  | 6. B |

| Chapters 14-17 | Chapters 18-21 | Chapters 22-24 |
|---|---|---|
| 1. C | 1. B | 1. D |
| 2. D | 2. A | 2. A |
| 3. C | 3. D | 3. C |
|  |  | 4. B |
|  |  | 5. C |
|  |  | 6. B |

# PREREADING VOCABULARY WORKSHEETS

# VOCABULARY - *The Scarlet Letter*

<u>Chapters 1-4</u>
Part I: Using Prior Knowledge and Contextual Clues

Below are the sentences in which the vocabulary words appear in the text. Read the sentence. Use any clues you can find in the sentence combined with your prior knowledge, and write what you think the underlined words mean in the space provided.

1. The founders of a new colony, whatever Utopia of human virtue and happiness they might originally project, have <u>invariably</u> recognized it among their earliest practical necessities to allot a portion of the virgin soil as a cemetery. . . .

2. Finding it so directly on the threshold of our narrative, which is now about to issue from that <u>inauspicious</u> portal, we could hardly do otherwise than pluck one of its flowers, and present it to the reader.

3. . . . that the mildest and the severest acts of public discipline were alike made <u>venerable</u> and awful.

4. The age had not so much refinement, that any sense of <u>impropriety</u> restrained the wearers of petticoat and farthingale from stepping forth into the public ways. . . .

5. Those who had before known her, . . . were astonished, and even startled, to perceive how her beauty shone out, and made a halo of the misfortune and <u>ignominy</u> in which she was enveloped.

6. Although, by a seemingly careless arrangement of his heterogeneous garb, he had endeavored to conceal or <u>abate</u> the peculiarity. . . .

7. It <u>irks</u> me, nevertheless, that the partner of her iniquity should not, at least, stand on the scaffold by her side.

8. . . . with the scarlet token of <u>infamy</u> on her breast . . .

Vocabulary Worksheet *Scarlet Letter* Chapters 1-4 Continued

Part II: Determining the Meaning -- Match the vocabulary words to their dictionary definitions.

___ 1. demeanor         A. lessen; reduce in amount or degree
___ 2. venerable        B. unfortunate; ill-omened
___ 3. ignominy         C. manner; way in which a person conducts himself
___ 4. inauspicious     D. evil fame or reputation
___ 5. impropriety      E. worthy of reverence or respect
___ 6. abate            F. something improper, incorrect; not appropriate
___ 7. irks             G. dishonor; infamy; disgraceful conduct
___ 8. infamy           H. annoys

Vocabulary - *The Scarlet Letter* Chapters 5-7

Part I: Using Prior Knowledge and Contextual Clues

Below are the sentences in which the vocabulary words appear in the text. Read the sentence. Use any clues you can find in the sentence combined with your prior knowledge, and write what you think the underlined words mean in the space provided.

1. But there is a fatality, a feeling so irresistible and <u>inevitable</u> that it has the force of doom, . . . .

2. It was as if a new birth . . . had converted the forest-land, still so <u>uncongenial</u> to every other pilgrim and wanderer, into Hester Prynne's wild and dreary, but life-long home.

3. She bore on her breast . . . a specimen of her delicate and imaginative skill, of which the dames of a court might gladly have availed themselves, to add the richer and more spiritual adornment of human <u>ingenuity</u> to their fabrics of silk and gold.

4. . . . even the silence of those with whom she came in contact, <u>implied</u>, and often expressed, that she was banished . . . .

5. . . . it seared Hester's bosom so deeply, that perhaps there was more truth in the rumor than our modern <u>incredulity</u> may be inclined to admit.

6. We have as yet hardly spoken of the infant; that little creature, whose innocent life had sprung, by the <u>inscrutable</u> decree of Providence, a lovely and immortal flower, out of the rank luxuriance of a guilty passion.

7. Pearl's aspect was <u>imbued</u> with a spell of infinite variety; in this one child there were many children . . . .

8. It was a look so intelligent, yet <u>inexplicable</u>, so perverse, sometimes so <u>malicious</u>, but generally accompanied by a wild flow of spirits . . .

9. Another and far more important reason than the delivery of a pair of embroidered gloves <u>impelled</u> Hester, at this time, to seek an interview with a personage of so much power

Vocabulary - *The Scarlet Letter* Chapters 5-7 Continued

Part II: Determining the Meaning -- Match the vocabulary words to their dictionary definitions.

___ 9. uncongenial     A. saturated; permeated
___ 10. inevitable     B. disbelief
___ 11. ingenuity     C. not possible to explain
___ 12. implied     D. not suitable; not agreeable
___ 13. incredulity     E. not able to be understood; mysterious
___ 14. inscrutable     F. unavoidable
___ 15. imbued     G. compelled; urged to action by moral pressure
___ 16. inexplicable     H. to express indirectly; hint; suggest
___ 17. impelled     I. inventive skill or imagination; cleverness

Vocabulary - *The Scarlet Letter* Chapters 8-10

Part I: Using Prior Knowledge and Contextual Clues
    Below are the sentences in which the vocabulary words appear in the text. Read the sentence. Use any clues you can find in the sentence combined with your prior knowledge, and write what you think the underlined words mean in the space provided.

1. . . . this badge hath taught me . . . lessons whereof my child may be the wiser and better, <u>albeit</u> they can profit nothing to myself.


2. The elders, the deacons, the motherly dames, and the young and fair maidens, of Mr. Dimmesdale's flock, were alike <u>importunate</u> that he should make trial of the physician's frankly offered skill. Mr. Dimmesdale gently repelled their <u>entreaties</u>.


3. Roger Chillingworth possessed all, or most, of the attributes above <u>enumerated</u>.


4. . . . it truly seemed that this <u>sagacious</u>, experienced, benevolent old physician . . . was the very man of all mankind to be constantly within reach of his voice.


5. He groped along as stealthily, with as cautious a tread, and as <u>wary</u> an outlook, as a thief entering a chamber where a man lies only half asleep . . . .


6. . . . Mr. Dimmesdale . . . would become vaguely aware that something <u>inimical</u> to his peace had thrust itself into relation with him.


7. Why should not the guilty ones sooner <u>avail</u> themselves of this unutterable solace?

Vocabulary - *The Scarlet Letter* Chapters 8-10 Continued

Part II: Determining the Meaning -- Match the vocabulary words to their dictionary definitions.

___ 18. albeit
___ 19. importunate
___ 20. entreaties
___ 21. enumerated
___ 22. sagacious
___ 23. wary
___ 24. inimical
___ 25. avail

A. wise
B. not conducive; harmful; adverse
C. stubbornly persistent in a request or demand
D. although
E. make use of; benefit
F. pleas; petitions; requests
G. listed
H. cautious

Vocabulary - *The Scarlet Letter* Chapters 11-13

Part I: Using Prior Knowledge and Contextual Clues

Below are the sentences in which the vocabulary words appear in the text. Read the sentence. Use any clues you can find in the sentence combined with your prior knowledge, and write what you think the underlined words mean in the space provided.

1. There were men, too, of a sturdier texture of mind than his, and endowed with a far greater share of shrewd, hard, iron, or granite understanding, which . . . constitutes a highly respectable, efficacious, and <u>unamiable</u> variety of the clerical species.

2. Had he told his hearers that he was altogether vile, a viler companion of the vilest, the worst of sinners, an abomination, a thing of unimaginable <u>iniquity</u> . . .

3. An unvaried <u>pall</u> of cloud muffled the whole expanse of sky from zenith to horizon.

4. We <u>impute</u> it, therefore, solely to the disease in his own eye and heart . . . .

5. His moral force was <u>abased</u> into more than childish weakness.

6. . . . society was inclined to show its former victim a more <u>benign</u> countenance than she cared to be favored with, or, perchance, than she deserved.

7. Thus, Hester Prynne, whose heart had lost its regular and healthy throb, wandered without a clew in the dark labyrinth of mind: now turned aside by an <u>insurmountable</u> precipice; now starting back from a deep chasm.

8. Finally, all other difficulties being <u>obviated</u>, woman cannot take advantage of these preliminary reforms, until she herself shall have undergone a still mightier change . . . .

Vocabulary - *The Scarlet Letter* Chapters 11-13 Continued

Part II: Determining the Meaning -- Match the vocabulary words to their dictionary definitions.

__ 26. unamiable      A. lowered in rank; humbled; humiliated
__ 27. iniquity      B. covering that darkens or obscures
__ 28. pall      C. not good natured; not agreeable
__ 29. impute      D. anticipated and disposed of effectively
__ 30. abased      E. sin; wickedness
__ 31. benign      F. to attribute
__ 32. insurmountable      G. of a kind disposition; gentle or mild
__ 33. obviated      H. not capable of being climbed or overcome

Vocabulary - *The Scarlet Letter* Chapters 14-17

Part I: Using Prior Knowledge and Contextual Clues
　　Below are the sentences in which the vocabulary words appear in the text. Read the sentence. Use any clues you can find in the sentence combined with your prior knowledge, and write what you think the underlined words mean in the space provided.

1. Yea, indeed!--he did not err!--there was a fiend at his elbow!

2. The unfortunate physician . . . lifted his hands with a look of horror, as if he had beheld some frightful shape, which he could not recognize, underline{usurping} the place of his own image in a glass.

3. . . . I shall stoop to implore thy mercy.

4. At first, as already told, she had flirted fancifully with her own image in a pool of water, beckoning the phantom forth, and . . . seeking a passage for herself into its sphere of impalpable earth and unattainable sky.

5. "And what reason is that?" asked Hester, half smiling at the absurd incongruity of the child's observation . . . .

6. She possessed affections, too, though hitherto acrid and disagreeable, as are the richest flavors of unripe fruit.

7. Here they sat down on a luxuriant heap of moss, which, at some epoch of the preceding century, had been a gigantic pine . . . .

Vocabulary - *The Scarlet Letter* Chapters 14-17 Continued

Part II: Determining the Meaning
    Match the vocabulary words to their dictionary definitions. If there are words for which you cannot figure out the definition by contextual clues and by process of elimination, look them up in a dictionary.

____ 34. err                      A. to entreat; plead; beg
____ 35. usurping             B. harsh; caustic; bitter
____ 36. implore              C. milestone; particular point in time
____ 37. impalpable         D. make a mistake
____ 38. incongruity         E. not matching
____ 39. acrid                 F. taking over
____ 40. epoch               G. not able to be touched

Vocabulary - *The Scarlet Letter* Chapters 18-21

Part I: Using Prior Knowledge and Contextual Clues

Below are the sentences in which the vocabulary words appear in the text. Read the sentence. Use any clues you can find in the sentence combined with your prior knowledge, and write what you think the underlined words mean.

1. "Hasten, Pearl; or I shall be angry with thee!" cried Hester Prynne, who, however <u>inured</u> to such behavior on the elf-child's part at other seasons, was naturally anxious for a more seemly deportment now.

2. But Pearl, not a whit startled at her mother's threats any more than <u>mollified</u> by her entreaties, now suddenly burst into a fit of passion . . . .

3. . . . the <u>intervening</u> space of a single day had operated on his consciousness like the lapse of years.

4. . . . my good word will go far towards gaining any strange gentleman a fair reception from yonder <u>potentate</u> you wot of!

5. I thank you, and can but <u>requite</u> your good deeds with my prayers.

6. Might there not be an irresistible desire to <u>quaff</u> a last, long, breathless draught of the cup of wormwood and aloes . . . .

7. It might be, on this one day, that there was an expression unseen before, nor, indeed, vivid enough to be detected now; unless some preternaturally gifted observer should have first read the heart, and have afterwards sought a corresponding development in the countenance a<u>nd mien</u>

Vocabulary - *The Scarlet Letter* Chapters 18-21 Continued

Part II: Determining the Meaning

Match the vocabulary words to their dictionary definitions. If there are words for which you cannot figure out the definition by contextual clues and by process of elimination, look them up in a dictionary.

___ 41. inured
___ 42. intervening
___ 43. mollified
___ 44. potentate
___ 45. requite
___ 46. quaff
___ 47. mien

A. repay
B. calmed; pacified
C. to have become used to something undesirable
D. one's bearing or manner; appearance
E. to drink heartily
F. coming between so as to hinder or modify
G. monarch; one who holds power or position over others

Vocabulary - *The Scarlet Letter* Chapters 22-24

Part I: Using Prior Knowledge and Contextual Clues

Below are the sentences in which the vocabulary words appear in the text. Read the sentence. Use any clues you can find in the sentence combined with your prior knowledge, and write what you think the underlined words mean in the space provided.

1. It is not for me to talk lightly of a learned and pious minister of the World, like the Reverend Mr. Dimmesdale!

2. There was a sense within her . . . that her whole orb of life, both before and after, was connected with this spot, as with the one point that gave it unity.

3. Hester's strong, calm, steadfastly enduring spirit almost sank, at last, on beholding this dark and grim countenance of an inevitable doom, which . . . showed itself, with an unrelenting smile, right in the midst of their path.

4. These . . . now thronged about Hester Prynne with rude and boorish intrusiveness.

5. . . . through the whole discourse, there had been a certain deep, sad undertone of pathos, which could not be interpreted otherwise than as the natural regret of one soon to pass away.

6. How feeble and pale he looked, amid all his triumph!

7. And now, almost imperceptible as were the latter steps of his progress, he had come opposite the well-remembered and weather-darkened scaffold . . . .

8. Surely, surely, we have ransomed one another, with all this woe!

Vocabulary - *The Scarlet Letter* Chapters 22-24 Continued

Part II: Determining the Meaning -- Match the vocabulary words to their dictionary definitions.

___ 48. pious
___ 49. orb
___ 50. unrelenting
___ 51. intrusiveness
___ 52. pathos
___ 53. amid
___ 54. imperceptible
___ 55. woe

A. not capable of being discerned by the senses or mind
B. deep sorrow; grief; misfortune
C. devout; religious
D. surrounded by; in the middle of
E. a compass of endeavor, influence or activity; sphere
F. coming in rudely or inappropriately; enter uninvited
G. not diminishing in speed, intensity or effort
H. a quality in something that arouses feelings of pity, sorrow, or sympathy

# VOCABULARY ANSWER KEY - *The Scarlet Letter*

| Chapters 1-4 | Chapters 5-7 | Chapters 8-10 | Chapters 11-13 |
|---|---|---|---|
| 1. C | 9. D | 18. D | 26. C |
| 2. E | 10. F | 19. C | 27. E |
| 3. G | 11. I | 20. F | 28. B |
| 4. B | 12. H | 21. G | 29. F |
| 5. F | 13. B | 22. A | 30. A |
| 6. A | 14. E | 23. H | 31. G |
| 7. H | 15. A | 24. B | 32. H |
| 8. D | 16. C | 25. E | 33. D |
|  | 17. G |  |  |

| Chapters 14-17 | Chapters 18-21 | Chapters 22-24 |
|---|---|---|
| 34. D | 41. C | 48. C |
| 35. F | 42. F | 49. E |
| 36. A | 43. B | 50. G |
| 37. G | 44. G | 51. F |
| 38. E | 45. A | 52. H |
| 39. B | 46. E | 53. D |
| 40. C | 47. D | 54. A |
|  |  | 55. B |

# DAILY LESSONS

# LESSON ONE

Objectives
1. To introduce the unit
2. To distribute books and other related materials

Activity #1

Divide your class into groups of four or five students. Each group's objective is to draw up a list of the ten most important laws/rules of our society (written or just understood). What ten rules, if we follow them, will keep us out of trouble?

When students have finished their work, compile a list of the ten best answers from all of the groups.

Transition: These are things we must do in our society. Let's turn back the hands of time to the 1600's. We're living in Puritan New England. What rules would we have to follow in a Puritan society?

Activity #2

Brainstorm a list as an entire class instead of in groups. Write the list on the board next to the present-day list. Compare and contrast the two lists. Discuss possible punishments today and in Puritan times for each of the various offenses. Note that the Puritans would use more corporal punishment (stocks in the town square, public ridicule, etc.)

**Transition:** The story we are about to read is about a woman and a man living in Boston in the 1600's who commit the sin of adultery. (Explain what that means if you think your students don't know.) The woman had an illegitimate child and was jailed for the crime/sin of adultery. She refused to tell the name of the man who fathered her child. This is the story of their lives following the woman's jail sentence.

Activity #3

Distribute the materials students will use in this unit. Explain in detail how students are to use these materials.

Study Guides  Students should read the study guide questions for each reading assignment prior to beginning the reading assignment to get a feeling for what events and ideas are important in the section they are about to read. After reading the section, students will (as a class or individually) answer the questions to review the important events and ideas from that section of the book. Students should keep the study guides as study materials for the unit test.

Vocabulary  Prior to reading a reading assignment, students will do vocabulary work related to the section of the book they are about to read. Following the completion of the reading of the book, there will be a vocabulary review of all the words used in the vocabulary assignments. Students should keep their vocabulary work as study materials for the unit test.

Reading Assignment Sheet  You need to fill in the reading assignment sheet to let students know by when their reading has to be completed. You can either write the assignment sheet up on a side blackboard or bulletin board and leave it there for students to see each day, or you can "ditto" copies for each student to have. In either case, you should advise students to become very familiar with the reading assignments so they know what is expected of them.

Extra Activities Center  The resource sections of this unit contain suggestions for an extra library of related books and articles in your classroom as well as crossword and word search puzzles. Make an extra activities center in your room where you will keep these materials for students to use. (Bring the books and articles in from the library and keep several copies of the puzzles on hand.) Explain to students that these materials are available for students to use when they finish reading assignments or other class work early.

Nonfiction Assignment Sheet  Explain to students that they each are to read at least one non-fiction piece from the in-class library at some time during the unit. Students will fill out a nonfiction assignment sheet after completing the reading to help you evaluate their reading experiences and to help the students think about and evaluate their own reading experiences.

Books  Each school has its own rules and regulations regarding student use of school books. Advise students of the procedures that are normal for your school.

# NONFICTION ASSIGNMENT SHEET
(To be completed after reading the required nonfiction article)

Name _____ Date _____

Title of Nonfiction Read _____

Written By _____ Publication Date _____

I. Factual Summary: Write a short summary of the piece you read.

II. Vocabulary
    1. With which vocabulary words in the piece did you encounter some degree of difficulty?

    2. How did you resolve your lack of understanding with these words?

III. Interpretation: What was the main point the author wanted you to get from reading his work?

IV. Criticism
    1. With which points of the piece did you agree or find easy to accept? Why?

    2. With which points of the piece did you disagree or find difficult to believe? Why?

V. Personal Response: What do you think about this piece? <u>OR</u> How does this piece influence your ideas?

## LESSON TWO

Objectives
    1. To do the prereading work for chapters 1-4
    2. To give students practice reading orally
    3. To evaluate students' oral reading

Activity #1

    Give students about 10 minutes or so at the beginning of the class to do the prereading work for chapters 1-4.

Activity #2

    Have students read chapters 1-4 of *The Scarlet Letter* out loud in class. You probably know the best way to get readers with your class; pick students at random, ask for volunteers, or use whatever method works best for your group. If you have not yet completed an oral reading evaluation for your students this marking period, this would be a good opportunity to do so. A form is included with this unit for your convenience.

    If students do not complete reading chapters 1-4 in class, they should do so prior to your next class meeting.

## LESSON THREE

Objectives
    1. To review the main events and ideas from chapters 1-4
    2. To preview the study questions for chapters 5-7
    3. To familiarize students with the vocabulary in chapters 5-7
    4. To read chapters 5-7

Activity #1

    Give students a few minutes to formulate answers for the study guide questions for chapters 1-4, and then discuss the answers to the questions in detail. Write the answers on the board or overhead transparency so students can have the correct answers for study purposes. *Note*: It is a good practice in public speaking and leadership skills for individual students to take charge of leading the discussions of the study questions. Perhaps a different student could go to the front of the class and lead the discussion each day that the study questions are discussed during this unit. Of course, the teacher should guide the discussion when appropriate and be sure to fill in any gaps the students leave.

Activity #2

    Give students about fifteen minutes to preview the study questions for chapters 5-7 of *The Scarlet Letter* and to do the related vocabulary work.

Activity #3

    Continue your oral reading evaluations using chapters 5-7 of *The Scarlet Letter*. Students should finish reading this assignment prior to your next class period.

# ORAL READING EVALUATION - *The Scarlet Letter*

Name _____ Class_____ Date _____

| SKILL | EXCELLENT | GOOD | AVERAGE | FAIR | POOR |
|---|---|---|---|---|---|
| Fluency | 5 | 4 | 3 | 2 | 1 |
| Clarity | 5 | 4 | 3 | 2 | 1 |
| Audibility | 5 | 4 | 3 | 2 | 1 |
| Pronunciation | 5 | 4 | 3 | 2 | 1 |
| _____ | 5 | 4 | 3 | 2 | 1 |
| _____ | 5 | 4 | 3 | 2 | 1 |

Total _____    Grade _____

Comments:

# LESSON FOUR

Objectives
1. To review the main ideas and events from chapters 5-7
2. To give students the opportunity to practice writing to persuade
3. To give the teacher an opportunity to evaluate each student's writing skills
4. To give students an opportunity to produce an error-free paper and to apply the teacher's suggestions
5. To assign the pre-reading activities and the reading of chapters 8-10

Activity #1
Review the answers for the study questions for chapters 5-7.

Activity #2
Distribute Writing Assignment #1 and discuss the directions in detail. Allow the remaining class time for students to complete the assignment. Collect the papers at the end of the class period.

Follow - Up: After you have graded the assignments, have a writing conference with the students. (This unit schedules one in Lesson Six.) After the writing conference, allow students to revise their papers using your suggestions and corrections. Give them about three days from the date they receive their papers to complete the revision. I suggest grading the revisions on an A-C-E scale (all revisions well-done, some revisions made, few or no revisions made). This will speed your grading time and still give some credit for the students' efforts.

Activity #3
Tell students that prior to the next class period they should have previewed the study questions for, done the vocabulary for and read chapters 8-10. If they have time after completing the writing assignment, they may begin this reading assignment in class.

# WRITING ASSIGNMENT #1 - *Scarlet Letter*

## PROMPT

At this point in your reading, you probably have some opinion about Hester's guilt, her punishment, and whether or not she should be allowed to keep Pearl.

Your assignment is to write a letter to Governor Bellingham regarding your opinion about what he should do about Hester.

## PREWRITING

If you have some difficulty forming an opinion, consider some of these issues: Should she keep or give up Pearl? Was making her wear the letter "A" a fair punishment? What punishment would you have thought appropriate for Hester, if any?

## DRAFTING

One way to structure your letter would be to make an **introductory paragraph** introducing yourself as a concerned citizen of Boston and stating your point. Follow that with a few paragraphs giving reasons for your point. (Each reason would be a **topic sentence**.) Fill in the paragraphs with **examples** supporting your reasons. Make a **concluding paragraph** thanking the governor for his time and his consideration of your opinions.

## PROMPT

When you finish the rough draft of your paper, ask a student who sits near you to read it. After reading your rough draft, he/she should tell you what he/she liked best about your work, which parts were difficult to understand, and ways in which your work could be improved. Reread your paper considering your critic's comments, and make the corrections you think are necessary.

## PROOFREADING

Do a final proofreading of your paper double-checking your grammar, spelling, organization, and the clarity of your ideas.

## LESSON FIVE

Objectives
   1. To read chapters 8-10
   2. To complete the prereading work for chapters 11-13
   3. To give students the opportunity to practice concentrating on reading silently

Activity

   Explain to students that prior to the next class period they should have completed reading through chapter 10 of *The Scarlet Letter* and should also have completed the prereading work (study question review and vocabulary work) for chapters 11-13. Give the students this class period to work on these two assignments.

## LESSON SIX

Objectives
   1. To review the main ideas of chapters 8-13
   2. To make sure students have done the required reading and prereading work from Lesson Five
   3. To preview the study questions for chapters 14-17
   4. To read chapters 14-17
   5. To discuss students' first writing assignment with them individually

Activity #1

   Quiz - Distribute quizzes and give students about 10 minutes to complete them.

Note: The quizzes may either be the short answer study guides or the multiple choice version. Have students exchange papers. Grade the quizzes as a class. Collect the papers for recording the grades. If you used the multiple choice version as a quiz, take a few minutes to discuss the answers for the short answer version if your students are using the short answer version for their study guides.

Activity #2

   Tell students to preview the study questions, do the vocabulary work for and read chapters 14-17. Tell students that this assignment should be completed prior to your next class meeting.

Activity #3

   While students are working on the assignment made in Activity #2, call students to your desk (or some other private area) to discuss their papers from Writing Assignment 1. A Writing Evaluation Form is included with this unit to help structure your conferences.

   After students have had a writing conference with you, they should return to their seats and begin working on their writing assignment revisions while your suggestions are fresh in their minds. Be sure to give students a day and a date for when their revisions are due.

WRITING EVALUATION - *The Scarlet Letter*

Name _____ Date _____

Writing Assignment #1 for the *Scarlet Letter* unit   Grade _____

Circle One For Each Item:

| | | |
|---|---|---|
| Letter Format: | correct | errors noted on paper |
| Character Analysis: | excellent | good   fair   poor |
| Grammar: | correct | errors noted on paper |
| Spelling: | correct | errors noted on paper |
| Punctuation: | correct | errors noted on paper |
| Legibility: | excellent | good   fair   poor |

Strengths:

Weaknesses:

Comments/Suggestions:

## LESSON SEVEN

Objectives
1. To review the main events of chapters 14-17
2. To complete the prereading work for chapters 18-21
3. To read chapters 18-21
4. To complete the oral reading evaluations

Activity #1
Do the study questions for chapters 14-17 with your class as you have done them for previous chapters.

Activity #2
Give students about ten or fifteen minutes to complete the prereading work for chapters 18-21.

Activity #3
Have your students read chapters 18-21 orally in class. If you have not yet done so, this is a good time to complete the oral reading evaluations. If students do not complete this assignment during class, they should complete it prior to your next class period.

## LESSON EIGHT

Objectives
1. To review the main ideas and events from chapters 18-21
2. To do the prereading work for chapters 22-24
3. To complete reading the novel

Activity #1
Do the study questions for chapters 18-21 as you have done the study questions for other chapters in the book.

Activity #2
Tell students that prior to your next class period they should have completed the prereading work for chapters 22-24 and should have completed reading the novel.

Give students the remainder of this class period to complete these assignments.

## LESSON NINE

Objectives
    1. To review the main ideas and events of chapters 22-24
    2. To review all of the vocabulary work done in this unit

Activity #1
    Discuss the answers to the study guide questions for chapters 22-24. Write the answers on the board for students to copy down for study use later.

Activity #2
    Choose one (or more) of the vocabulary review activities listed below and spend your class period as directed in the activity. Some of the materials for these review activities are located in the Extra Activities Packet in this unit.

### VOCABULARY REVIEW ACTIVITIES

1. Divide your class into two teams and have an old-fashioned spelling or definition bee.

2. Give each of your students (or students in groups of two, three or four) a *The Scarlet Letter* Vocabulary Word Search Puzzle. The person (group) to find all of the vocabulary words in the puzzle first wins.

3. Give students a *The Scarlet Letter* Vocabulary Word Search Puzzle without the word list. The person or group to find the most vocabulary words in the puzzle wins.

4. Use a *The Scarlet Letter* Vocabulary Crossword Puzzle. Put the puzzle onto a transparency on the overhead projector (so everyone can see it), and do the puzzle together as a class.

5. Give students a *The Scarlet Letter* Vocabulary Matching Worksheet to do.

6. Divide your class into two teams. Use the *Scarlet Letter* vocabulary words with their letters jumbled as a word list. Student 1 from Team A faces off against Student 1 from Team B. You write the first jumbled word on the board. The first student (1A or 1B) to unscramble the word wins the chance for his/her team to score points. If 1A wins the jumble, go to student 2A and give him/her a definition. He/she must give you the correct spelling of the vocabulary word which fits that definition. If he/she does, Team A scores a point, and you give student 3A a definition for which you expect a correctly spelled matching vocabulary word. Continue giving Team A definitions until some team member makes an incorrect response. An incorrect response sends the game back to the jumbled-word face off, this time with students 2A and 2B. Instead of repeating giving definitions to the first few students of each team, continue with the student after the one who gave the last incorrect response on the team. For example, if Team B wins the jumbled-word face-off, and student 5B gave the last incorrect answer for Team B, you would start this round of definition questions with student 6B, and so on. The team with the most points wins!

# LESSON TEN

## Objectives
1. To prepare students for an in-depth discussion of the novel
2. To give students the opportunity to do any research necessary
3. To give students the opportunity to choose materials for their nonfiction reading assignments or for their own personal reading enjoyment

## Activity #1
Take your class to the library. Make sure they take their books and materials on which to write their compositions.

Choose the questions from the Extra Discussion Questions/Writing Assignments which seem most appropriate for your students. Assign one question to each student and give students this class period to work on formulating their answers in a written form.

## Activity #2
If students complete the assignment early, they should use the library's resources to check out books for their personal reading enjoyment or articles for their nonfiction reading assignment that goes along with this unit.

NOTE: Advise students that in the next class period they will be expected to give their answers to the Extra Discussion Questions orally in front of the class and to lead any discussion that arises relating to their answers.

# EXTRA WRITING ASSIGNMENTS/DISCUSSION QUESTIONS - *The Scarlet Letter*

Interpretation

1. Explain what point of view Nathaniel Hawthorne used in *The Scarlet Letter* and explain why he chose to use it.

2. If you were to rewrite *The Scarlet Letter* as a play, where would you start and end each act? Explain why.

3. What is the function of the character of Mr. Wilson in the novel?

4. Define "sin" as it is set forth in *The Scarlet Letter*.

5. Compare and contrast Dimmesdale and Chillingworth.

6. Write a synopsis of the life of any of the historical figures mentioned in *The Scarlet Letter*.

7. What are the main conflicts in the story, and how is each resolved?

Critical

8. Explain the meaning and the importance of the passages involving Mistress Hibbins.

9. Are Rev. Dimmesdale's actions believably motivated? Explain why or why not.

10. Explain the importance of the setting in *The Scarlet Letter*. Could this story have been set in a different time and place and still have the same effect?

11. Evaluate Nathaniel Hawthorne's style of writing. How does it contribute to the value of the novel?

12. Explain the meaning and the importance of the three scaffold scenes.

13. What is Pearl's use as a character? Hester and Dimmesdale could have committed adultery without producing Pearl. Why did Hawthorne include her?

14. How is *The Scarlet Letter* a story about good versus evil?

15. Explain the change of attitude by the townspeople towards Hester. What was it, how did it take place, and why did Hawthorne include it?

16. Why is this book considered to be a "classic"?

17. What are the main themes of the book?

*The Scarlet Letter* Extra Discussion Questions page 2

18. Are the characters in *The Scarlet Letter* stereotypes? If so, explain why Nathaniel Hawthorne used stereotypes. If not, explain how the characters merit individuality.

19. Why are there so many references made to witchcraft and devil worshiping?

20. Was Hester's affair with Dimmesdale justifiable since her husband was missing and presumed dead? Give your own answer, and then answer as if you were a Puritan.

Critical/Personal Response

21. Could the events of this novel realistically happen today? Explain why or why not.

22. Many descriptions of Pearl in the book cast her as a most strange child, yet at the end of the book she seems to have gone on to lead a very normal life. Reconcile these facts.

23. Did Hester deserve the punishment she got? Fully explain your answer.

24. Suppose Hester would tell about the events of the story a few years after it happened. What do you think she would say?

25. Was Dimmesdale's situation as bad as he thought it was?

26. Why didn't Dimmesdale come forth earlier?

Personal Response

27. Did you enjoy reading *The Scarlet Letter*? Why or why not?

28. If abortion were an option for Hester, do you think she would have chosen it?

29. Was Dimmesdale a good minister? Explain why or why not.

30. The Puritans tried to legislate morality. Are there any laws in our country which attempt to do the same? Are they successful?

31. Are there groups of people similar to the Puritans today? Who are they and what effect do they have on society?

32. Would you have liked being an early settler in New England?

33. Hester and Dimmesdale both seemed to need to feel a sense of punishment for their sin/crime. Do you think most people feel that way? That is, do most people feel the need to be punished for bad actions they consciously commit?

*The Scarlet Letter* Extra Discussion Questions page 3

34. How long should someone have to "pay" for his or her crimes? Is there a point in time when all should be forgiven and society should give a person a fresh start?

35. What would the world be like if we all had to wear a sign stating our worst faults: "I'm a liar," "I cheat," "I am bitter," "I am prejudiced," "I am lazy," etc.?

36. Most people have a sense of "right" and "wrong"; we usually make a conscious decision about whether we are going to do the "right" thing or the "wrong" thing. Why should people try to do the "right" thing?

<u>Quotations</u>

1. But the point which drew all eyes . . . was that scarlet letter, so fantastically embroidered and illuminated upon her bosom. It had the effect of a spell, taking her out of the ordinary relations with humanity, and enclosing her in a sphere by herself.

2. Here, she said to herself, had been the scene of her guilt, and here should be the scene of her earthly punishment; and so, perchance, the torture of her daily shame would at length purge her soul, and work out another purity than that which she had lost; more saint-like, because the result of martyrdom.

3. Day after day, she looked fearfully into the child's expanding nature, ever dreading to detect some dark and wild peculiarity, that should correspond with the guiltiness to which she owed her being.

4. There is one worse than even the polluted priest! That old man's revenge has been blacker than my sin. He has violated, in cold blood, the sanctity of a human heart.

5. The future is yet full of trial and success. There is happiness to be enjoyed! There is good to be done! Exchange this false life of thine for a true one.

6. "Mother," said she, "was that the same minister that kissed me by the brook?"

*The Scarlet Letter* Extra Discussion Questions page 4

7. Finding [a rose bush] so directly on the threshold of our narrative, which is now about to issue from that inauspicious portal, we could hardly do otherwise than pluck one of its flowers, and present it to the reader. It may serve, let us hope, to symbolize some sweet moral blossom, that may be found along the track, or relieve the darkening close of a tale of human frailty and sorrow.

8. When the young woman--the mother of this child-- stood fully revealed before the crowd, it seemed to be her first impulse to clasp the infant closely to her bosom; not so much by an impulse of motherly affection, as that she might thereby conceal a certain token, which was wrought or fastened into her dress. In a moment, however, wisely judging that one token of her shame would but poorly serve to hide another, she took the baby on her arm, and, with a burning blush, and yet a haughty smile, and a glance that would not be abashed, looked around at her townspeople and neighbors.

9. "Why dost thou smile so at me?" inquired Hester, troubled at the expression of his eyes. "Art thou like the Black Man that haunts the forest round about us? Hast thou enticed me into a bond that will prove the ruin of my soul?"
"Not thy soul," he answered, with another smile, "No, not thine!"

10. "There is no path to guide us out of this dismal maze!"

11. "Ha, tempter! Methinks thou art too late!" answered the minister, encountering his eye, fearfully, but firmly.

12. Surely, surely, we have ransomed one another, with all this woe!

13. "Hadst thou sought the whole earth over," said he, looking darkly at the clergyman, "there was no one place so secret,--no high place nor lowly place, where thou couldst have escaped me,--save on this very scaffold!"

*The Scarlet Letter* Extra Discussion Questions page 5

14. "Be true! Be true! Be true! Show freely to the world, if not your worst, yet some trait whereby the worst may be inferred!"

15. . . . the scarlet letter ceased to be a stigma which attracted the world's scorn and bitterness, and became a type of something to be sorrowed over, and looked upon with awe, yet with reverence, too.

16. "On a field, sable, the letter A, gules."

## LESSON ELEVEN

Objectives
    1. To help students better understand the novel
    2. To check students' work from Lesson Ten
    3. To give students the opportunity to practice public speaking

Activity

    Have individual students (one-by-one) go to the front of the class to give their answers to the questions they were assigned in Lesson Ten. Students should give their answers to their questions and lead any discussions that arise from their answers. You, the teacher, should be sure to jump in to the discussion to make sure that all the important points you are looking for are covered.

## LESSON TWELVE

Objectives
    1. Students will investigate the text for symbols Hawthorne used and determine some reasonable theory as to what each symbol may mean
    2. Students will work together in small groups to improve their group interaction skills and accomplish Objective 1
    3. Students will report their findings during a follow-up group discussion

Activity #1

    Divide the class into groups of four students. Divide the number of groups you have into the number of chapters in *The Scarlet Letter* (24) to determine the number of chapters each group will have to cover. Assign specific chapters to each group of students. Explain that they are to work together to find any symbols in their assigned chapters and determine some theory as to what each symbol might mean.

    When they get together in their groups, the students' first task will be to divide their chapters into sections, one section for each group member. Each student should investigate his assigned section, looking for any symbols and jot down the symbol, as well as the page and paragraph number for reference. Students will then compare and share notes, working together to compile a complete list of symbols. They should then go through the list and work together to determine the possible meanings of each symbol. At least one group member should be appointed to jot down these ideas, which will be reported in Activity 2.

Activity #2

    Have each group report its findings, giving the list of symbols and their possible meanings orally. Discuss the symbols as necessary and make a list of the findings on the board for all students to copy. At the end of all of the reports, students should have an accurate record of symbolism in *The Scarlet Letter*. Tell students to keep their lists and to be sure to bring them to the next class meeting.

# LESSON THIRTEEN

Objectives
1. To give students the opportunity to write to inform
2. To follow up on the discussions held in Lesson Twelve
3. To give students the opportunity to digest and use the information they learned in Lesson Twelve
4. To get a sample of students' writing to evaluate

Activity #1

Distribute Writing Assignment #2. Discuss the directions in detail and give students the remainder of this class period to work on this assignment. Be sure to tell students when their compositions will be due.

Follow-Up: Follow up as in Writing Assignment 1, allowing students to correct their errors and turn in the revision for credit. A good time for your next writing conferences would be the day following the unit test.

Activity #2

If students finish writing early, they should continue working on their nonfiction reading assignments or do a vocabulary or unit review worksheet.

# WRITING ASSIGNMENT #2 - *The Scarlet Letter*

## PROMPT

You have spent some time working with symbolism in *The Scarlet Letter*. Now it is time to organize it, put it in perspective, and to "lay it out," so-to-speak, in writing.

Your assignment is to write a composition in which you succinctly but thoroughly explain the use of symbolism in *The Scarlet Letter*.

## PREWRITING

The best place to start is to review your notes from the discussions held in the last class period. What one statement can you make about all those different symbols in the book? (Some questions to think about are: What effect did the symbols have on your understanding and/or enjoyment of the book? Were the symbols effectively used by the author? Could the element of symbolism have been handled better in the book? How or why not?) When you formulate your one statement, write it down.

After you have formulated your one statement, think of the things that made you believe your statement was true. What evidence or support is there for your statement? Write down the things that support your statement.

## DRAFTING

With your class notes and the notes you have just made, you are ready to begin writing. Make an introductory paragraph in which you introduce the one main statement you formulated above. Follow that paragraph with paragraphs that support your one main statement. Use one of each of your items of evidence or support as the topic for each of the paragraphs in the body of your paper. Finish out your paper with a concluding paragraph in which you tie up and/or summarize the ideas you have presented in your paper.

## PROMPT

When you finish the rough draft of your paper, ask a student who sits near you to read it. After reading your rough draft, he/she should tell you what he/she liked best about your work, which parts were difficult to understand, and ways in which your work could be improved. Reread your paper considering your critic's comments, and make the corrections you think are necessary.

## PROOFREADING

Do a final proofreading of your paper double-checking your grammar, spelling, organization, and the clarity of your ideas.

# LESSON FOURTEEN

Objectives
    1. To further develop the theme of morality/making moral choices
    2. To show students that all people make moral decisions every day
    3. To give students the opportunity to evaluate their own moral values

NOTE: There are many commercially prepared games on the market which pose moral questions. If you prefer, you could use one of those already prepared games.

Activity #1
    Ask students to take out a piece of paper and write down two or three situations in which they have had to make a moral decision; a decision between "right" and "wrong." Students do not have to put their names on these papers. If you wish, you could make this assignment more impersonal by having students write down two situations in which someone they know (or a generic "someone") had to make a moral decision. Collect the papers for use in Activity #2.

    NOTE: Some suggestions or examples of situations are given following this lesson.

Activity #2
    Tell students to take out a sheet of paper. Using the situations students provided in Activity #1, ask students to make their own decisions about what they would do in each situation. For example, read the situation: "You are working on a part-time job. You see your co-worker, whom you like, taking money from the cash register and putting it in her pocket." Then, ask the appropriate question: "Would you tell the boss?" Give students ample time to write down their answers for each situation.

Activity #3
    When you have used up all of the situations given, go back through the questions again. This time, ask for a show of hands for each possible response. (In the case of the example above, ask for a show of hands for how many students *would* tell the boss and then a show of hands for how many students *would not* tell the boss.) Discuss the complexities of the situations as is necessary.

Activity #4
    Remind students that their nonfiction reports will be done in the next class period.

# SAMPLE MORAL CHOICE SITUATIONS - *The Scarlet Letter*

1. You're in a store. You spot a small item you really want, but you don't have enough money to pay for it. There is no alarm tag on the item, so if you take it, no alarm will sound as you exit the store. You look around. There is only one other person in the store, and the clerk is busy ringing up his sale. Would you slip the item into your coat pocket?

2. You parents have told you to go straight home after school, but your friends want you to go out with them for a little while. Your parents won't be home for at least three hours. Would you go with your friends or go home?

3. You forgot to study for your science test. The paper of the person next to you is easily legible with just a glance or two. Would you peek and cheat or not?

4. You saw your best friend's girl/boy friend on a date with someone else. Your friend thinks the girl/boy friend is only seeing him/her. Do you tell your friend that his/her girl/boy friend is cheating on him/her?

5. You got into trouble at school, but no one at school called your parents to tell them. After dinner one of your parents asks you how things are going at school. Do you tell the parent about the incident of trouble?

6. You and an acquaintance have a huge argument at lunchtime. You are absolutely furious. Your acquaintance is in your next class. Before class starts, he/she had dumped his/her stuff on a desk and has gone to the hallway. You see something of importance, though of no great monetary value, in plain sight in his/her pile of belongings on the desk. You know that he/she would be hurt by missing that item (perhaps a homework paper or project, a favorite baseball card, a letter from a girl/boy friend, etc.) Would you take the item out of spite?

7. You see two class mates cheating on a test. Do you tell the teacher?

8. You see a team member taking drugs prior to a game. He/she does not know that you have seen him/her. Would you tell the coach?

# LESSON FIFTEEN

## Objectives
1. To widen the breadth of students' knowledge about the topics discussed or touched upon in *The Scarlet Letter*
2. To check students' nonfiction reading assignments

## Activity #1

Ask each student to give a brief oral report about the nonfiction work he/she read for the nonfiction reading assignment. Your criteria for evaluating this report will vary depending on the level of your students. You may wish for students to give a complete report without using notes of any kind, or you may want students to read directly from a written report, or you may want to do something in between these two extremes. Just make students aware of your criteria in ample time for them to prepare their reports.

Start with one student's report. After that, ask if anyone else in the class has read on a topic related to the first student's report. If no one has, choose another student at random. After each report, be sure to ask if anyone has a report related to the one just completed. That will help keep a continuity during the discussion of the reports.

# LESSON SIXTEEN

Objectives
> 1. To give students the opportunity to look at real life crimes and to think about what punishments are appropriate for each
> 2. To carry the theme of crime and punishment beyond the pages of the book

NOTE: The best way to get the information you need to carry out this lesson is to invite a local criminal trial attorney to your class. Explain to him/her that your class has just read *The Scarlet Letter*, a book about a Puritan woman who committed adultery and had to wear a letter "A" on her clothing as a part of her punishment. Explain that you are trying to carry the theme of crime and punishment out of the pages of the book into a real world situation. Ask the attorney if he/she would come to your class to give the class details about several of his/her "favorite" cases, describing the crimes committed, letting the students give their responses about what punishments they think would have been appropriate, and then telling students what actual punishments were handed out by the courts.

If you can't get an attorney to come to your class, you or some of your students could go to the library to find information about famous trials that have taken place, and use those situations as the basis for your discussions.

This lesson is planned assuming you are able to find an attorney (or a judge or a politician who was an attorney!)

Activity #1
Introduce the attorney to your students, giving them a bit of background about him/her. Explain that he/she is in your class today to take the theme of crime and punishment out of the long-ago Puritan world in the text pages to real life and present day.

Explain that the attorney is going to talk about some real-life cases, giving enough information that they can make a decision about what punishment they think is appropriate for the accused. Ask students to give the attorney their full attention and to pay attention to the details of the cases so they can make informed decisions about the punishments. Turn your class over to the attorney so he/she can tell the first case. After each case, ask students what they think an appropriate punishment would be. Have the attorney tell what happened to the defendant.

Activity #2
If you have time left over after the attorney has discussed all the cases for which he/she is prepared, give students the opportunity to ask any general questions they want of the attorney (with his/her permission to do so, of course).

NOTE: A good extra writing activity in conjunction with this lesson is to have students write a letter of thanks to the attorney.

## LESSON SEVENTEEN

Objectives:
1. To give students the opportunity to write to express their own personal opinions
2. To make students think about the reality of jail sentences and punishments in general
3. To give the teacher the opportunity to evaluate students' writing
4. To carry the theme of crime and punishment not only out of the text and into real life, but into students' personal lives

Activity #1
    Distribute Writing Assignment 3. Discuss the directions in detail and give students the remainder of this class period to work on this assignment.

Follow-up One good follow-up activity for this writing assignment is to have someone from a local correctional institution come to your class to describe exactly what it is like to be in jail (a daily schedule, duties, rights and/or privileges, hazards, etc.).

# WRITING ASSIGNMENT #3 - *The Scarlet Letter*

## PROMPT

You have been to a party at the home of an acquaintance. Some people at the party were drinking alcohol; some were doing drugs. You were not necessarily involved with either of these activities; nevertheless, you were attending the party. The police came in and arrested all nine of you who were in the room. You were carted off to jail to wait for a bond review. You are sitting in jail. What are your thoughts?

## PREWRITING

To help you get started, consider some of these issues: What things are foremost in your mind? Will parental or peer reaction be a factor in your thoughts? What is your actual physical state: Are you hot, cold, uncomfortable, confused, angry ...? What are your surroundings like now? What are your concerns about your surroundings? What are your thoughts about your future? Will this change any of your plans for the future? What are your prospects?

## DRAFTING

Consider this assignment more of a piece of creative writing than a formal, essay-type composition. If you feel comfortable writing in a structured way, feel free to group your thoughts in the traditional way using one paragraph to express your feelings about one aspect of your incarceration, another paragraph to express your feelings about another aspect of your incarceration, etc. You don't have to adhere to the usual topic-sentence-followed-by-further-support-for-the-topic-sentence routine. Also, if you prefer, you may use a stream of consciousness-type of format, writing as things occur to you. The point is to actually put yourself into the situation and fully explore your thoughts and feelings about it.

## PROMPT

Beware. Clarity may be your key enemy in this assignment. Make your thoughts clear so that your reader will understand what you are thinking about and how you feel. One way to check this is to have a student who sits near you read your composition when you have completed a rough draft. After reading your rough draft, he/she should tell you what he/she liked best about your work, which parts were difficult to understand, and ways in which your work could be improved. Reread your paper considering your critic's comments, and make the corrections you think are necessary.

## PROOFREADING

Do a final proofreading of your paper double-checking your grammar, spelling, organization, and especially the clarity of your ideas.

# LESSON EIGHTEEN

Objective
    To review the main ideas presented in *The Scarlet Letter*

Activity #1
    Choose one of the review games/activities included in the packet and spend your class period as outlined there. Some materials for these activities are located in the Extra Activities Packet section of this unit.

Activity #2
    Remind students that the Unit Test will be in the next class meeting. Stress the review of the Study Guides and their class notes as a last minute, brush-up review for homework.

REVIEW GAMES/ACTIVITIES - *The Scarlet Letter*

1. Ask the class to make up a unit test for *The Scarlet Letter*. The test should have 4 sections: matching, true/false, short answer, and essay. Students may use 1/2 period to make the test and then swap papers and use the other 1/2 class period to take a test a classmate has devised. (open book) You may want to use the unit test included in this packet or take questions from the students' unit tests to formulate your own test.

2. Take 1/2 period for students to make up true and false questions (including the answers). Collect the papers and divide the class into two teams. Draw a big tic-tac-toe board on the chalk board. Make one team X and one team O. Ask questions to each side, giving each student one turn. If the question is answered correctly, that students' team's letter (X or O) is placed in the box. If the answer is incorrect, no mark is placed in the box. The object is to get three marks in a row like tic-tac-toe. You may want to keep track of the number of games won for each team.

3. Take 1/2 period for students to make up questions (true/false and short answer). Collect the questions. Divide the class into two teams. You'll alternate asking questions to individual members of teams A & B (like in a spelling bee). The question keeps going from A to B until it is correctly answered, then a new question is asked. A correct answer does not allow the team to get another question. Correct answers are +2 points; incorrect answers are -1 point.

4. Have students pair up and quiz each other from their study guides and class notes.

5. Give students a *The Scarlet Letter* crossword puzzle to complete.

6. Divide your class into two teams. Use the *Scarlet Letter* crossword words with their letters jumbled as a word list. Student 1 from Team A faces off against Student 1 from Team B. You write the first jumbled word on the board. The first student (1A or 1B) to unscramble the word wins the chance for his/her team to score points. If 1A wins the jumble, go to student 2A and give him/her a clue. He/she must give you the correct word which matches that clue. If he/she does, Team A scores a point, and you give student 3A a clue for which you expect another correct response. Continue giving Team A clues until some team member makes an incorrect response. An incorrect response sends the game back to the jumbled-word face off, this time with students 2A and 2B. Instead of repeating giving clues to the first few students of each team, continue with the student after the one who gave the last incorrect response on the team. For example, if Team B wins the jumbled-word face-off, and student 5B gave the last incorrect answer for Team B, you would start this round of clue questions with student 6B, and so on.

# UNIT TESTS

# SHORT ANSWER UNIT TEST 1 - *The Scarlet Letter*

I. Short Answer

1. What emblem did Hester have to wear? Why was she sentenced to wear it?

2. What was the relationship between Hester and Roger Chillingworth?

3. Why did Hester go to see Governor Bellingham?

4. What does Rev. Dimmesdale's congregation think of him? Why is that ironic?

5. Why do Hester and Pearl go to the forest?

6. How did Rev. Mr. Dimmesdale's attitude change after he decided to leave Boston with Hester?

7. What did Mr. Dimmesdale tell the people of New England before he died?

*The Scarlet Letter* Short Answer Unit Test 1 page 2

II. Briefly explain the significance of the following quotations:

1. But the point which drew all eyes . . . was that scarlet letter, so fantastically embroidered and illuminated upon her bosom. It had the effect of a spell, taking her out of the ordinary relations with humanity, and enclosing her in a sphere by herself.

2. Here, she said to herself, had been the scene of her guilt, and here should be the scene of her earthly punishment; and so, perchance, the torture of her daily shame would at length purge her soul, and work out another purity than that which she had lost; more saint-like, because the result of martyrdom.

3. Day after day, she looked fearfully into the child's expanding nature, ever dreading to detect some dark and wild peculiarity, that should correspond with the guiltiness to which she owed her being.

4. There is one worse than even the polluted priest! That old man's revenge has been blacker than my sin. He has violated, in cold blood, the sanctity of a human heart.

5. The future is yet full of trial and success. There is happiness to be enjoyed! There is good to be done! Exchange this false life of thine for a true one.

*The Scarlet Letter* Short Answer Unit Test 1 page 3

6. "Mother," said she, "was that the same minister that kissed me by the brook?"

7. "Hadst thou sought the whole earth over," said he, looking darkly at the clergyman, "there was no one place so secret,--no high place nor lowly place, where thou couldst have escaped me,--save on this very scaffold!"

8. "Be true! Be true! Be true! Show freely to the world, if not your worst, yet some trait whereby the worst may be inferred!"

9. . . . the scarlet letter ceased to be a stigma which attracted the world's scorn and bitterness, and became a type of something to be sorrowed over, and looked upon with awe, yet with reverence, too.

10. "On a field, sable, the letter A, gules."

*The Scarlet Letter* Short Answer Unit Test 1 page 4

III. Composition

"Finding [this rose-bush] so directly on the threshold of our narrative . . . we could hardly do otherwise than pluck one of its flowers, and present it to the reader. It may serve, let us hope, to symbolize some sweet moral blossom that may be found along the track, or relieve the darkening close of a tale of human frailty and sorrow."

1. What "sweet moral blossom" were we intended to find in *The Scarlet Letter*? Answer in detail using support from the events or ideas in the text.

2. Why is *The Scarlet Letter* a "tale of human frailty and sorrow" and why does it have a "darkening close"? Explain fully.

*The Scarlet Letter* Short Answer Unit Test 1 page 5

IV. Vocabulary

Listen to the vocabulary word and spell it. After you have spelled all the words, go back and write down the definitions.

1.

2.

3.

4.

5.

6.

7.

8.

9.

10.

# SHORT ANSWER UNIT TEST 2 - *The Scarlet Letter*

I. Short Answer

1. Identify Hester Prynne, Pearl, Rev. Mr. Dimmesdale and Roger Chillingworth.

2. What was the relationship between Hester and Roger Chillingworth?

3. Describe Pearl.

4. What convinced the Governor to let Hester keep Pearl?

5. Why did Mr. Dimmesdale rush from the room to end the conversation he had with Roger Chillingworth?

6. Why do Hester and Pearl go to the forest?

7. What did Hester have to do by the brook before Pearl would come across?

8. What shocking news did the commander of the Bristol ship bring Hester?

*The Scarlet Letter* Short Answer Test 2 page 2
II. Briefly explain the significance of the following quotations:

1. Finding [a rose bush] so directly on the threshold of our narrative, which is now about to issue from that inauspicious portal, we could hardly do otherwise than pluck one of its flowers, and present it to the reader. It may serve, let us hope, to symbolize some sweet moral blossom, that may be found along the track, or relieve the darkening close of a tale of human frailty and sorrow.

2. When the young woman--the mother of this child-- stood fully revealed before the crowd, it seemed to be her first impulse to clasp the infant closely to her bosom; not so much by an impulse of motherly affection, as that she might thereby conceal a certain token, which was wrought or fastened into her dress. In a moment, however, wisely judging that one token of her shame would but poorly serve to hide another, she took the baby on her arm, and, with a burning blush, and yet a haughty smile, and a glance that would not be abashed, looked around at her townspeople and neighbors.

3. "Why dost thou smile so at me?" inquired Hester, troubled at the expression of his eyes. "Art thou like the Black Man that haunts the forest round about us? Hast thou enticed me into a bond that will prove the ruin of my soul?"
"Not thy soul," he answered, with another smile, "No, not thine!"

4. "There is no path to guide us out of this dismal maze!"

*The Scarlet Letter* Short Answer Test 2 page 3

5. "Ha, tempter! Methinks thou art too late!" answered the minister, encountering his eye, fearfully, but firmly.

6. Surely, surely, we have ransomed one another, with all this woe!

7. "Hadst thou sought the whole earth over," said he, looking darkly at the clergyman, "there was no one place so secret,--no high place nor lowly place, where thou couldst have escaped me,--save on this very scaffold!"

8. "Be true! Be true! Be true! Show freely to the world, if not your worst, yet some trait whereby the worst may be inferred!"

9. . . . the scarlet letter ceased to be a stigma which attracted the world's scorn and bitterness, and became a type of something to be sorrowed over, and looked upon with awe, yet with reverence, too.

*The Scarlet Letter* Short Answer Test 2 page 4
III. Composition

> How could *The Scarlet Letter* be seen as a story of good versus evil? Explain your answer in detail using events and ideas from the text.

*The Scarlet Letter* Short Answer Test 2 page 5

IV. Vocabulary

Listen to the vocabulary words and spell them.
After you have spelled all the words, go back and write down the definitions.

1.

2.

3.

4.

5.

6.

7.

8.

9.

10.

# ANSWER KEY: SHORT ANSWER UNIT TEST 2 *The Scarlet Letter*

The short answer questions are taken directly from the study guides.
If you need to look up the answers, you will find them in the study guide section.

Answers to the composition questions will vary depending on your
class discussions and the level of your students.

For the vocabulary section of the test, choose ten of the
words from the vocabulary lists to dictate to your students.

# ADVANCED SHORT ANSWER UNIT TEST - *The Scarlet Letter*

I. Character Identification

1. Compare and contrast Dimmesdale and Chillingworth.

2. Explain the use and importance of Pearl in the story.

3. Give a complete character analysis of Hester.

4. Explain the use and importance of Chillingworth in the story.

*The Scarlet Letter* Advanced Short Answer Test page 2

II. Quotations
    Explain the significance of the following quotations.

1. Finding [a rose bush] so directly on the threshold of our narrative, which is now about to issue from that inauspicious portal, we could hardly do otherwise than pluck one of its flowers, and present it to the reader. It may serve, let us hope, to symbolize some sweet moral blossom, that may be found along the track, or relieve the darkening close of a tale of human frailty and sorrow.

2. When the young woman--the mother of this child-- stood fully revealed before the crowd, it seemed to be her first impulse to clasp the infant closely to her bosom; not so much by an impulse of motherly affection, as that she might thereby conceal a certain token, which was wrought or fastened into her dress. In a moment, however, wisely judging that one token of her shame would but poorly serve to hide another, she took the baby on her arm, and, with a burning blush, and yet a haughty smile, and a glance that would not be abashed, looked around at her townspeople and neighbors.

3. But the point which drew all eyes . . . was that scarlet letter, so fantastically embroidered and illuminated upon her bosom. It had the effect of a spell, taking her out of the ordinary relations with humanity, and enclosing her in a sphere by herself.

4. "Be true! Be true! Be true! Show freely to the world, if not your worst, yet some trait whereby the worst may be inferred!"

*The Scarlet Letter* Advanced Short Answer Test  page 3

5. "Ha, tempter! Methinks thou art too late!" answered the minister, encountering his eye, fearfully, but firmly.

6. Surely, surely, we have ransomed one another, with all this woe!

7. "Hadst thou sought the whole earth over," said he, looking darkly at the clergyman, "there was no one place so secret,--no high place nor lowly place, where thou couldst have escaped me,--save on this very scaffold!"

8. "On a field, sable, the letter A, gules."

9. . . . the scarlet letter ceased to be a stigma which attracted the world's scorn and bitterness, and became a type of something to be sorrowed over, and looked upon with awe, yet with reverence, too.

*The Scarlet Letter* Advanced Short Answer Test  page 4

III. Vocabulary

Listen to the vocabulary words and write them down. Later go back and write a composition in which you use all of the vocabulary words. The composition must in some way relate to *The Scarlet Letter*.

# MULTIPLE CHOICE UNIT TEST 1 - *The Scarlet Letter*

I. Matching

1. Letter      A. The Governor

2. Witch      B. Dimmesdale to Pearl

3. Washes      C. Feel sorry for an action

4. Sin      D. A woman who works for the devil

5. Move      E. What Hester must wear

6. Hester      F. She promises not to reveal Chillingworth's identity

7. Repent      G. Something which represents something else

8. Bellingham      H. He brought Hester bad news

9. Doctor      I. Jail

10. Symbol      J. Pearl's father

11. Confess      K. What Dimmesdale did just before he died

12. Needlework      L. Chillingworth's occupation in Boston

13. Dimmesdale      M. Sin of which Hester & Dimmesdale were guilty

14. Commander      N. Hester suggests Dimmesdale should do this

15. Temptation      O. A morally wrong thing to do

16. Revenge      P. Author

17. Prison      Q. Hester's means of supporting herself and Pearl

18. Hawthorne      R. Dimmesdale felt this to do bad things; a luring

19. Adultery      S. Chillingworth seeks this against Dimmesdale

20. Father      T. Pearl --- off Dimmesdale's kiss in the brook

*The Scarlet Letter* Multiple Choice Test 1 Page 2

II. Multiple choice

1. For what did the letter A stand?
    a. Alone
    b. Adultery
    c. Adopted
    d. Aspersion

2. What was the relationship between Hester and Roger Chillingworth?
    a. They were divorced.
    b. They were just married.
    c. They were married but had been separated.
    d. They were in love.

3. Hester is released from prison. Why doesn't she run away to a different settlement?
    a. She is not allowed to under the terms of her release.
    b. She loves Rev. Dimmesdale and must remain near to him.
    c. Pearl is too young to travel.
    d. She feels her soul may be purged clean if she remains living there, disgraced.

4. Why did Hester go to see Governor Bellingham?
    a. To plead for her life
    b. To tell him Roger's true identity
    c. To plead to keep Pearl
    d. To tell him that Rev. Dimmesdale was the other sinner

5. What convinced the Governor to let Hester keep Pearl?
    a. Hester would constantly remind Pearl of the consequences of sin.
    b. Rev. Dimmesdale promised to watch the mother and child closely & report anything that might interest the governor
    c. Hester agreed to allow Chillingworth live with her and Pearl, so they could all be a "real family."
    d. It was just a whim, as was his customary way of making decisions.

6. Who is the leech?
    a. Dimmesdale
    b. Hester
    c. Pearl
    d. Chillingworth

*The Scarlet Letter* Multiple Choice Test 1 Page 3

7. What does Rev. Dimmesdale's congregation think of him?
	a. They think he's a pitiful minister.
	b. They think he's practically a saint.
	c. They think he's a horrible sinner.
	d. They think he's a weak man who succumbed to the temptations of life.

8. Why do Hester and Pearl go to the forest?
	a. To enjoy nature's solitude
	b. To pick flowers
	c. To pray
	d. To intercept Dimmesdale

9. When Mr. Dimmesdale finds out that Roger Chillingworth is out for revenge, he knows his religious career in Boston will be at an end and his life will be miserable. What does Hester suggest?
	a. She suggests a plot to get rid of Chillingworth.
	b. She suggests that Dimmesdale should take Pearl and go away.
	c. She suggests that Dimmesdale should go away, taking her and Pearl, too.
	d. She suggests that Dimmesdale should stay and face his punishment as she has done, that, in doing so, his soul might also be cleansed before his life ends.

10. How did Rev. Mr. Dimmesdale's attitude change after he decided to leave Boston with Hester?
	a. Felt better
	b. Had more energy
	c. Felt temptation to do bad things
	d. All of the above

11. What news did the commander of the Bristol ship bring Hester?
	a. The ship's departure would be delayed by at least three weeks.
	b. Chillingworth had taken Pearl on board the ship *Venturer*.
	c. Dimmesdale had already left on board the ship *Venturer*.
	d. Chillingworth had booked passage on the Bristol ship.

12. What did Mr. Dimmesdale tell the people of New England before he died?
	a. He confessed that he was the one who had sinned with Hester.
	b. He told them to beware, to be watchful of their own souls; even the most pious among them is easy prey to temptation.
	c. He asked their eternal forgiveness and their pity upon Hester and Pearl.
	d. All of the above

*The Scarlet Letter* Multiple Choice Test 1 Page 4
III. Vocabulary

1. Abate — A. Wise
2. Entreaties — B. Pleas; petitions; requests
3. Impropriety — C. Surrounded by; in the middle of
4. Amid — D. Unfortunate; ill-omened
5. Orb — E. Compelled; urged to action by moral pressure
6. Sagacious — F. Saturated; permeated
7. Irks — G. Devout; religious
8. Benign — H. Anticipated and disposed of effectively
9. Epoch — I. Something improper; incorrect; not appropriate
10. Incredulity — J. Disbelief
11. Inevitable — K. Milestone; particular point in time
12. Incongruity — L. Annoys
13. Imbued — M. Something that doesn't match
14. Inauspicious — N. Unavoidable
15. Impelled — O. Not conducive; harmful; adverse
16. Obviated — P. Worthy of reverence or respect
17. Pious — Q. Make a mistake
18. Venerable — R. Of a kind disposition; gentle or mild
19. Inimical — S. A compass of endeavor, influence or activity; sphere
20. Err — T. Lessen; reduce in amount or degree

*The Scarlet Letter* Multiple Choice Test 1 Page 5

IV. Composition

"Finding [this rose-bush] so directly on the threshold of our narrative . . . we could hardly do otherwise than pluck one of its flowers, and present it to the reader. It may serve, let us hope, to symbolize some sweet moral blossom that may be found along the track, or relieve the darkening close of a tale of human frailty and sorrow."

1. What "sweet moral blossom" were we intended to find in *The Scarlet Letter*? Answer in detail using support from the events or ideas in the text.

2. Why is *The Scarlet Letter* a "tale of human frailty and sorrow" and why does it have a "darkening close"? Explain fully.

# MULTIPLE CHOICE UNIT TEST 2 - *The Scarlet Letter*

I. Matching

| | | |
|---|---|---|
| 1. Letter | | A. Jail |
| 2. Witch | | B. What Hester must wear |
| 3. Washes | | C. Author |
| 4. Sin | | D. Pearl --- off Dimmesdale's kiss in the brook |
| 5. Move | | E. Dimmesdale to Pearl |
| 6. Hester | | F. The Governor |
| 7. Repent | | G. Something which represents something else |
| 8. Bellingham | | H. He brought Hester bad news |
| 9. Doctor | | I. She promises not to reveal Chillingworth's identity |
| 10. Symbol | | J. Pearl's father |
| 11. Rose | | K. Could be found just outside the prison |
| 12. Needlework | | L. Sin of which Hester & Dimmesdale were guilty |
| 13. Dimmesdale | | M. Chillingworth's occupation in Boston |
| 14. Commander | | N. Hester suggests Dimmesdale should do this |
| 15. Temptation | | O. A morally wrong thing to do |
| 16. Revenge | | P. Dimmesdale felt this to do bad things; a luring |
| 17. Prison | | Q. Hester's means of supporting herself and Pearl |
| 18. Hawthorne | | R. Feel sorry for an action |
| 19. Adultery | | S. Chillingworth seeks this against Dimmesdale |
| 20. Father | | T. A woman who works for the devil |

*The Scarlet Letter* Multiple Choice Test 2 Page 2

II. Multiple choice

1. For what did the letter A stand?
    a. Aspersion
    b. Adultery
    c. Adopted
    d. Alone

2. What was the relationship between Hester and Roger Chillingworth?
    a. They were divorced
    b. They were married but had been separated.
    c. They were just married.
    d. They were in love.

3. Hester is released from prison. Why doesn't she run away to a different settlement?
    a. She feels her soul may be purged clean if she remains living there, disgraced.
    b. She loves Rev. Dimmesdale and must remain near to him.
    c. Pearl is too young to travel.
    d. She is not allowed to under the terms of her release.

4. Why did Hester go to see Governor Bellingham?
    a. To plead for her life
    b. To tell him that Rev. Dimmesdale was the other sinner
    c. To tell him Roger's true identity
    d. To plead to keep Pearl

5. What convinced the Governor to let Hester keep Pearl?
    a. Hester would constantly remind Pearl of the consequences of sin.
    b. Hester agreed to allow Chillingworth live with her and Pearl, so they could all be a "real family."
    c. Rev. Dimmesdale promised to watch the mother and child closely & report anything that might interest the governor
    d. It was just a whim, as was his customary way of making decisions.

6. Who is the leech?
    a. Pearl
    b. Hester
    c. Dimmesdale
    d. Chillingworth

*The Scarlet Letter* Multiple Choice Test 2 Page 3

7. What does Rev. Dimmesdale's congregation think of him?
    a. They think he's a horrible sinner.
    b. They think he's practically a saint.
    c. They think he's a pitiful minister.
    d. They think he's a weak man who succumbed to the temptations of life.

8. Why do Hester and Pearl go to the forest?
    a. To intercept Dimmesdale
    b. To pick flowers
    c. To pray
    d. To enjoy nature's solitude

9. When Mr. Dimmesdale finds out that Roger Chillingworth is out for revenge, he knows his religious career in Boston will be at an end and his life will be miserable. What does Hester suggest?
    a. She suggests that Dimmesdale should stay and face his punishment as she has done, that, in doing so, his soul might also be cleansed before his life ends.
    b. She suggests that Dimmesdale should take Pearl and go away.
    c. She suggests that Dimmesdale should go away, taking her and Pearl, too.
    d. She suggests a plot to get rid of Chillingworth.

10. How did Rev. Mr. Dimmesdale's attitude change after he decided to leave Boston with Hester?
    a. Had more energy
    b. Felt better
    c. Felt temptation to do bad things
    d. All of the above

11. What news did the commander of the Bristol ship bring Hester?
    a. Dimmesdale had already left on board the ship *Venturer*.
    b. Chillingworth had booked passage on the Bristol ship.
    c. The ship's departure would be delayed by at least three weeks.
    d. Chillingworth had taken Pearl on board the ship *Venturer*.

12. What did Mr. Dimmesdale tell the people of New England before he died?
    a. He asked their eternal forgiveness and their pity upon Hester and Pearl.
    b. He told them to beware, to be watchful of their own souls; even the most pious among them is easy prey to temptation.
    c. He confessed that he was the one who had sinned with Hester.
    d. All of the above

*The Scarlet Letter* Multiple Choice Test 2 Page 4

III. Vocabulary

1. Abate — A. Disbelief
2. Entreaties — B. Unfortunate; ill-omened
3. Impropriety — C. Surrounded by; in the middle of
4. Amid — D. Pleas; petitions; requests
5. Orb — E. Annoys
6. Sagacious — F. Devout; religious
7. Irks — G. Saturated; permeated
8. Benign — H. Anticipated and disposed of effectively
9. Epoch — I. Milestone; particular point in time
10. Incredulity — J. Wise
11. Inevitable — K. Something improper; incorrect; not appropriate
12. Incongruity — L. Compelled; urged to action by moral pressure
13. Imbued — M. Something that doesn't match
14. Inauspicious — N. Make a mistake
15. Impelled — O. Not conducive; harmful; adverse
16. Obviated — P. Worthy of reverence or respect
17. Pious — Q. A compass of endeavor, influence or activity; sphere
18. Venerable — R. Of a kind disposition; gentle or mild
19. Inimical — S. Unavoidable
20. Err — T. Lessen; reduce in amount or degree

*The Scarlet Letter* Multiple Choice Test 2 Page 5

IV. Composition

>How could *The Scarlet Letter* be seen as a story of good versus evil? Explain your answer in detail using events and ideas from the text.

ANSWER SHEET - *The Scarlet Letter*
Multiple Choice Unit Tests

| I. Matching | II. Multiple Choice | III. Vocabulary |
|---|---|---|
| 1. ___ | 1. ___ | 1. ___ |
| 2. ___ | 2. ___ | 2. ___ |
| 3. ___ | 3. ___ | 3. ___ |
| 4. ___ | 4. ___ | 4. ___ |
| 5. ___ | 5. ___ | 5. ___ |
| 6. ___ | 6. ___ | 6. ___ |
| 7. ___ | 7. ___ | 7. ___ |
| 8. ___ | 8. ___ | 8. ___ |
| 9. ___ | 9. ___ | 9. ___ |
| 10. ___ | 10. ___ | 10. ___ |
| 11. ___ | 11. ___ | 11. ___ |
| 12. ___ | 12. ___ | 12. ___ |
| 13. ___ | | 13. ___ |
| 14. ___ | | 14. ___ |
| 15. ___ | | 15. ___ |
| 16. ___ | | 16. ___ |
| 17. ___ | | 17. ___ |
| 18. ___ | | 18. ___ |
| 19. ___ | | 19. ___ |
| 20. ___ | | 20. ___ |

# ANSWER KEY - *The Scarlet Letter*
## Multiple Choice Unit Tests

Test 1 answers are in the left hand column. Test 2 answers are in the right hand column.

| I. Matching | | II. Multiple Choice | | III. Vocabulary | |
|---|---|---|---|---|---|
| 1. E | B | 1. B | B | 1. T | T |
| 2. D | T | 2. B | C | 2. B | D |
| 3. T | D | 3. A | D | 3. I | K |
| 4. O | O | 4. D | C | 4. C | C |
| 5. N | N | 5. A | A | 5. S | Q |
| 6. F | I | 6. D | D | 6. A | J |
| 7. C | R | 7. B | B | 7. L | E |
| 8. A | F | 8. A | D | 8. R | R |
| 9. L | M | 9. C | C | 9. K | I |
| 10. G | G | 10. D | D | 10. J | A |
| 11. K | K | 11. B | D | 11. N | S |
| 12. Q | Q | 12. C | A | 12. M | M |
| 13. J | J | | | 13. F | G |
| 14. H | H | | | 14. D | B |
| 15. R | P | | | 15. E | L |
| 16. S | S | | | 16. H | H |
| 17. I | A | | | 17. G | F |
| 18. P | C | | | 18. P | P |
| 19. M | L | | | 19. O | O |
| 20. B | E | | | 20. Q | N |

# UNIT RESOURCE MATERIALS

# BULLETIN BOARD IDEAS - *The Scarlet Letter*

1. Save one corner of the board for the best of students' *Scarlet Letter* writing assignments.

2. Title the board *The Scarlet Letter*. Cut out a large, red letter A. Place it in the center of the board. Around the A, write (or put up cut out letters for each character's name. Take yarn or string and attach the strings from the A out to each character's name. Arrange the names so you can fill in the yarn to make a spider's web to symbolize that the characters are all tied together by the scarlet letter (Hester's sin/crime of adultery).

3. Make a bulletin board which explores the separation of church and state. Use it as a springboard for discussion about that topic in relationship to the novel.

4. Take one of the word search puzzles from the extra activities packet and with a marker copy it over in a large size on the bulletin board. Write the clue words to find to one side. Invite students prior to and after class to find the words and circle them on the bulletin board.

5. Do a bulletin board about careers in law, law enforcement, justice system, and/or religion.

6. Following (or in conjunction with) the activities and assignments relating to symbolism, create (or have students create) a bulletin board relating to the symbols in *The Scarlet Letter*. Designing a bulletin board might be a good, short, small group, follow-up activity.

7. Post articles about famous trials that have taken place (or trials that are currently taking place).

8. Divide your board into six sections--one section for each of the six themes that the groups discuss in Lesson Twelve. In the appropriate board sections, post articles and/or photos which illustrate each of the themes.

9. Write several of the most significant quotations from the book onto the board on brightly colored paper.

10. Make a bulletin board about the Puritans and use it as a part of your introductory lesson. Better yet, create it using student suggestions from the introductory activity in Lesson One.

11. Make a bulletin board listing the vocabulary words for this unit. As you complete sections of the novel and discuss the vocabulary for each section, write the definitions on the bulletin board. (If your board is one students face frequently, it will help them learn the words.)

# EXTRA ACTIVITIES

One of the difficulties in teaching a novel is that all students don't read at the same speed. One student who likes to read may take the book home and finish it in a day or two. Sometimes a few students finish the in-class assignments early. The problem, then, is finding suitable extra activities for students.

The best thing I've found is to keep a little library in the classroom. For this unit on *The Scarlet Letter*, you might check out from the school library other related books and articles about the Puritans, how our justice system works, careers in the justice system or in religion, accounts of trials that have taken place, separation of church and state, attempts to legislate morality, society's views towards immorality, witchcraft, importance of morals in a society, or crimes and punishments.

Other things you may keep on hand are puzzles. WeI have made some relating directly to *The Scarlet Letter* for you. Feel free to duplicate them.

Some students may like to draw. You might devise a contest or allow some extra-credit grade for students who draw characters or scenes from *The Scarlet Letter*. Note, too, that if the students do not want to keep their drawings you may pick up some extra bulletin board materials this way. If you have a contest and you supply the prize (a CD or something like that perhaps), you could, possibly, make the drawing itself a non-refundable entry fee.

The pages which follow contain games, puzzles and worksheets. The keys, when appropriate, immediately follow the puzzle or worksheet. There are two main groups of activities: one group for the unit; that is, generally relating to *The Scarlet Letter*, and another group of activities related to the *Scarlet Letter* vocabulary.

Directions for these games, puzzles and worksheets are self-explanatory. The object here is to provide you with extra materials you may use in any way you choose.

# MORE ACTIVITIES - *The Scarlet Letter*

1. Pick a chapter or scene with a great deal of dialogue and have the students act it out on a stage. (Perhaps you could assign various scenes to different groups of students so more than one scene could be acted and more students could participate.)

2. Discuss the idea of the separation of church and state.

3. Show the film *The Scarlet Letter* after you have completed reading the novel in class. Have students evaluate the movie and compare/contrast it with the book. If the students have tried writing a chapter into a scene in a play, you may wish to discuss how the problems they encountered in changing the form were handled in the movie.

4. Have students design a book cover (front and back and inside flaps) for *The Scarlet Letter*.

5. Have students design a bulletin board (ready to be put up; not just sketched) for *The Scarlet Letter*.

6. Have students go through and find all the references to historical figures in *The Scarlet Letter*, and have students investigate each thoroughly.

7. Read "The Custom House" section of the book and discuss its relevance to the main story of *The Scarlet Letter*.

8. Hold a trial of your own for Hester. Have your class work out the whole scenario and write it as a play.

9. Have students rewrite a synopsis of the story from Hester's point of view. (They should pretend to be Hester talking, explaining the events of this story to her when she is older.)

10. Have your students wear something obvious which sets them apart from the remainder of the student population at your school for one day (perhaps a Puritan costume or something like that). Spend the next class period discussing how being different made them feel, and have them write a paper about their experiences.

11. Have students research famous trial cases, lawyers or judges.

12. Research about and discuss the selection of and current members of the U. S. Supreme Court.

# WORD SEARCH - *The Scarlet Letter*

All words in this list are associated with *The Scarlet Letter*. The words are placed backwards, forward, diagonally, up and down. The included words are listed below the word search.

```
K Q Q R S S S Q G R C F X R J L S H M D T X F C
T A T T W Y W A D C O C T V R A J F F N I M F L
L S B A M E X E R X O S H A I P G O N Y V E N V
B E L L I N G H A M O V E N N Y R P G D N I S T
K R E G E A C N M P O P T H R E I I L T W L H Z
J M I C S L R A E E R R J E S H D O S W U V W C
J H C S H T N E L V T O T T S A F M K O H D S T
Z Y A K T D E A P E E L M S Q F W R S C N E R H
M P B W E O D M L E U R E I A B O N T A R J T L
M L M R T S L R P D N F F C S W N I B U R R O D
N X S E E H A E A T N T S A E E W S T E O B B L
T J V M T C O R T O A Q N L T S U P T W M B C F
T P M S S E Q R C T W T D M G H I S G Y C F N H
R I D O C T O R N Z E E I R C R E N S B R O O K
D F C Y D L G R J E E R H O C H I R K K V L R K
J R T D W M N N F N F T Z S N L H X G V C K H P
N F R S G S K F Q T N R T H L W T N K H Y N Q R
C O N G R E G A T I O N W I C H U R C H M H C M
X X T X K R S F T Y S V H Z W T Q G K P B V M B
X Y B Y H Y H G P H C C V D G C F F B M M L L F
```

| | | | |
|---|---|---|---|
| ABLE | DIES | METEOR | SAINT |
| ADULTERY | DIMMESDALE | MOVE | SCAFFOLD |
| ARMOR | DOCTOR | NEEDLEWORK | SCARLET |
| BELLINGHAM | FATHER | PASSAGE | SCRIPTURES |
| BRISTOL | FOREST | PEARL | SHIP |
| BROOK | HAWTHORNE | PRISON | SIN |
| CHILLINGWORTH | HESTER | PROMISE | SOULS |
| CHURCH | HUSBAND | PRYNNE | SYMBOL |
| COMMANDER | LAWS | REPENT | TEMPTATION |
| CONFESS | LEECH | REVENGE | WASHES |
| CONGREGATION | LETTER | ROSE | WITCH |

# CROSSWORD - *The Scarlet Letter*

# CROSSWORD CLUES - *Scarlet Letter*

## ACROSS
1. Place where Pearl washed off D's kiss
3. Governor
8. Spirits; preachers try to save them
10. A morally wrong thing to do
11. Deep sorrow; grief; misfortune
12. A woman who works for the devil
13. Hester's illegitimate daughter
16. Sin of which Hester & D. were guilty
17. *The ---- Letter*
21. Cautious
22. Surrounded by; in the middle of
26. Expressed indirectly; hinted; suggested
28. Make a mistake
31. Chillingworth booked --- on the Bristol ship
34. Congregation's opinion of Dimmesdale
35. Dimmesdale to Pearl
37. To drink heartily
39. Place on which Dimmesdale confessed
42. Chillingworth seeks this against D
43. She must wear the letter "A"
44. To admit guilt
45. Lessen; reduce in amount or degree

## DOWN
2. Flower growing outside the prison
3. Commander of the --- ship brought Hester news
4. Hester's means of supporting herself & Pearl
5. Author
6. It made a sign in the sky
7. Chillingworth to Hester
8. Sea transportation
9. Something that represents something else
13. Hester's last name
14. Hester saw a distorted "A" in it
15. Rules and regulations
18. Hester's husband
19. Feel sorry for an action
20. Dimmesdale felt this to do bad things; a luring
23. Dimmesdale does this after confessing
24. Of a kind disposition; gentle or mile
25. Jail
27. Chillingworth
29. Pearl's father
30. Place of worship
31 Hester made one to C. -- to not reveal his identity
32. Bible
33. Some people said Hester's "A" stood for this
36. Pearl --- off Dimmesdale's kiss in the brook
38. Hester & Pearl went there to intercept Dimmesdale
40. Hester suggests D should do this & take her & Pearl along
41. One's bearing or manner; appearance

# CROSSWORD ANSWER KEY - *The Scarlet Letter*

|   | B | R | O | O | K |   |   | B | E | L | L | I | N | G | H | A | M |   |   | H |   |   |
|---|---|---|---|---|---|---|---|---|---|---|---|---|---|---|---|---|---|---|---|---|---|---|
|   |   | O |   |   |   |   |   | R |   |   |   | E |   | A |   | E |   | S | O | U | L | S |
|   |   | S |   |   |   | S | I | N |   | W | O | E |   | W | I | T | C | H |   | S |   | Y |
| P | E | A | R | L |   |   | S |   |   |   | D |   | T |   | E |   | I |   | B |   |   | M |
| R |   | R |   | A | D | U | L | T | E | R | Y |   | L |   | H |   | O |   | P |   | A | B |
| Y |   | M |   | W |   |   | O |   |   |   | E |   | O |   | R |   |   |   |   |   | N | O |
| N |   | O |   | S | C | A | R | L | E | T |   |   | W | A | R | Y |   | A | M | I | D | L |
| N |   | R |   | H |   |   | E |   |   | E |   |   | O |   | N |   |   | D |   |   | B |   |
| E |   |   | P |   | I |   | P |   |   | M |   |   | R |   | E |   | I | M | P | L | I | E | D |
|   | E | R | R |   | L |   | E |   |   | P |   | K |   |   | E |   |   | E |   | E |   | N |   |
| D |   |   | I |   | L |   | N |   |   | T |   | C |   | P | A | S | S | A | G | E |   | I |   |
| I |   | S | A | I | N | T |   | F | A | T | H | E | R |   | C |   | B |   | C |   |   | G |   |
| M |   |   | O |   | N |   |   |   | T |   | U |   | O |   | R |   | L |   | H |   |   | N |   |
| M |   |   | N |   | G |   |   |   | I |   | R |   | M |   | I |   | E |   |   |   |   |   |   |
| E |   | W |   | W |   |   |   |   | O |   | C |   | I |   | P |   |   |   | Q | U | A | F | F |
| S | C | A | F | F | O | L | D |   | N |   | H |   | S |   | T |   | M |   |   |   |   | O |   |
| D |   | S |   | R |   |   | M |   |   |   | E |   | U |   | O |   |   |   |   |   |   | R |   |
| A |   | H |   | T |   |   | I |   |   |   |   |   | R | E | V | E | N | G | E |   |   | E |   |
| L |   | E |   |   | H | E | S | T | E | R |   |   |   |   | E |   | E |   |   |   |   | S |   |
| E |   | S |   |   |   |   | N |   | C | O | N | F | E | S | S |   | A | B | A | T | E |   |   |

# MATCHING QUIZ/WORKSHEET 1 - *The Scarlet Letter*

___ 1. Souls      A. Chillingworth to Hester

___ 2. Sin      B. A morally wrong thing to do

___ 3. Doctor      C. Place of worship

___ 4. Needlework      D. Governor

___ 5. Move      E. Chillingworth

___ 6. Repent      F. Chillingworth's occupation in Boston

___ 7. Saint      G. Pearl -- off Dimmesdale's kiss in the brook

___ 8. Confess      H. Spirits; preachers try to save them

___ 9. Father      I. Feel sorry for an action

___ 10. Bellingham      J. A woman who works for the devil

___ 11. Rose      K. Hester suggests Dimmesdale should do this & take her & Pearl

___ 12. Leech      L. Chillingworth booked --- on the Bristol ship

___ 13. Hawthorne      M. Author

___ 14. Washes      N. To admit guilt

___ 15. Husband      O. She must wear a letter "A"

___ 16. Witch      P. Flower growing outside the prison

___ 17. Church      Q. Dimmesdale to Pearl

___ 18. Passage      R. Commander of the -- ship brought Hester news

___ 19. Hester      S. Congregation's opinion of Dimmesdale

___ 20. Bristol      T. Hester's means of supporting herself & Pearl

MATCHING QUIZ/WORKSHEET 2 - *The Scarlet Letter*

___ 1. Promise             A. Hester's means of supporting herself & Pearl

___ 2. Father              B. Something which represents something else

___ 3. Bellingham          C. Place on which Dimmesdale confessed

___ 4. Witch               D. Commander of the --- ship brought Hester news

___ 5. Move                E. Some people said Hester's "A" stood for this

___ 6. Bristol             F. Governor

___ 7. Sin                 G. She must wear the letter "A"

___ 8. Chillingworth       H. Hester saw a distorted "A" in it

___ 9. Symbol              I. Author

___ 10. Saint              J. Hester & Pearl intercept Dimmesdale there

___ 11. Scaffold           K. Illegitimate daughter of Hester

___ 12. Needlework         L. Congregation's opinion of Dimmesdale

___ 13. Congregation       M. Bible

___ 14. Hester             N. Hester suggests Dimmesdale should do this & take her and Pearl along

___ 15. Scriptures         O. Hester made one to Chillingworth -- to not reveal his identity

___ 16. Armor              P. Parishioners

___ 17. Pearl              Q. Dimmesdale to Pearl

___ 18. Hawthorne          R. A morally wrong thing to do

___ 19. Forest             S. Hester's husband

___ 20. Able               T. A woman who works for the devil

# KEY: MATCHING QUIZ/WORKSHEETS - *The Scarlet Letter*

| Worksheet 1 | Worksheet 2 |
|---|---|
| 1. H | 1. O |
| 2. B | 2. Q |
| 3. F | 3. F |
| 4. T | 4. T |
| 5. K | 5. N |
| 6. I | 6. D |
| 7. S | 7. R |
| 8. N | 8. S |
| 9. Q | 9. B |
| 10. D | 10. L |
| 11. P | 11. C |
| 12. E | 12. A |
| 13. M | 13. P |
| 14. G | 14. G |
| 15. A | 15. M |
| 16. J | 16. H |
| 17. C | 17. K |
| 18. L | 18. I |
| 19. O | 19. J |
| 20. R | 20. E |

# REVIEW GAME #7 CLUE SHEET - *The Scarlet Letter*

| SCRAMBLED | WORD | CLUE |
|---|---|---|
| KORBO | BROOK | Place where Pearl washed off D's kiss |
| ENATMTPOIT | TEMPTATION | Dimmesdale felt this to do bad things; a luring |
| ANROETHWH | HAWTHORNE | Author |
| TERLTE | LETTER | "A" for example |
| MMSEIALEDD | DIMMESDALE | Pearl's father |
| TEFRHA | FATHER | Dimmesdale to Pearl |
| EROS | ROSE | Flower growing outside the prison |
| WRDLEOENKE | NEEDLEWORK | Hester's work |
| OMEV | MOVE | Hester suggests Dimmesdale should & take her and Pearl |
| MDCMERANO | COMMANDER | Brought Hester news that Chillingworth had booked passage |
| IPTRSCESRU | SCRIPTURES | Bible readings |
| GHTNLRHICLOWI | CHILLINGWORTH | Hester's husband |
| SEASHW | WASHES | Pearl --- off D's kiss |
| BAEL | ABLE | Some said H's "A" stood for this |
| MORRA | ARMOR | Hester saw a distorted "A" in it |
| RLEPA | PEARL | Illegitimate daughter of Hester |
| UNAHSDB | HUSBAND | Chillingworth to Hester |
| TESFRO | FOREST | H & P intercept D there |
| SPRONI | PRISON | Jail |
| NGOEGRINAOCT | CONGREGATION | Parishioners |
| ENPRNY | PRYNNE | Hester's last name |
| HCIWT | WITCH | A woman who works for the devil |
| RSPIMEO | PROMISE | Hester made one to Chillingworth not to reveal his identity |
| HPSI | SHIP | Sea transportation |
| NGEVEER | REVENGE | C seeks this against D |
| REHSET | HESTER | She must wear the letter "A" |
| NSI | SIN | A morally wrong thing to do |
| UCCHRH | CHURCH | Place of worship |
| ALSW | LAWS | Rules & regulations |
| TRMEEO | METEOR | It made a sign in the sky |
| IESD | DIES | Dimmesdale does this after confessing |
| MHIGNBEALL | BELLINGHAM | Governor |
| TCODRO | DOCTOR | Chillingworth's profession in Boston |
| NTAIS | SAINT | Congregation's opinion of D |

# VOCABULARY RESOURCE MATERIALS

# VOCABULARY WORD SEARCH - *The Scarlet Letter*

All words in this list are associated with *The Scarlet Letter* with an emphasis on the vocabulary words for the unit. The words are placed backwards, forward, diagonally, up and down. The included words are listed below the word search.

```
X H R A X N W D R F V C M W S W Y V N D W E Z G
I X Q R V D G O E D N H L M Q T E E Q N N A Q I
E N T R E A T I E S U O I P G N I P R U S U R C
T M T R C M I L N P A M G M E M G E M G A K G Y
W J U R X Z L L K E P B S R P U R E B S S F I P
M N I D U E S E P E B B A O N U R E U L I N F Z
I D I Z P S T G R A R B R R N A T O Q G A R K D
F M P M K A I C X O L T E A T A I E N U S B N X
A W I M B S E V K E U L M E T C G O S A I T Y W
S Y L A O P P I E N E I D N A I M P E D E T I C
B M T H L M F A N A H E G N I I R E L I M E M
D W T I H B L T T B E T A T N C O T B U P G E H
L A B W U Y E I L Q O S E Y I L A A Q A Q P C D
P L L E X N N E F P N R S O P I T I L Z T O D P
E Z D H K G E D B I V B U M V I N P J R P E M G
M V P K S T L G F E E S I B V I A F N E I Y L J
P F Z N J V G X N W L D O E L B F W A L V L M Z
L A C I M I N I B I N L N N L D R W P M G H R P
M L K R S C N P S H L I N E J F G M P M Y J Z N
I N C O N G R U I T Y E L B A C I L P X E N I M
```

| | | | |
|---|---|---|---|
| ABASED | IMBUED | INGENUITY | PIOUS |
| ABATE | IMPALPABLE | INIMICAL | POTENTATE |
| ACRID | IMPELLED | INIQUITY | QUAFF |
| ALBEIT | IMPERCEPTIBLE | INTERVENING | REQUITE |
| AMID | IMPLIED | INTRUSIVENESS | SAGACIOUS |
| AVAIL | IMPLORE | INURED | UNAMIABLE |
| BENIGN | IMPORTUNATE | IRKS | UNRELENTING |
| DEMEANOR | IMPUTE | MIEN | USURPING |
| ENTREATIES | INAUSPICIOUS | MOLLIFIED | VENERABLE |
| ENUMERATED | INCONGRUITY | OBVIATED | WARY |
| EPOCH | INEVITABLE | ORB | WOE |
| ERR | INEXPLICABLE | PALL | |
| IGNOMINY | INFAMY | PATHOS | |

# VOCABULARY CROSSWORD - *The Scarlet Letter*

# VOCABULARY CROSSWORD CLUES - *Scarlet Letter*

## ACROSS
2. Something improper; not appropriate
7. Make a mistake
9. Harsh; caustic; bitter
12. Lessen; reduce in amount or degree
14. A compass of endeavor, influence or activity
15. Surrounded by; in the middle of
16. Milestone; particular point in time
17. To attribute
20. Saturated; permeated
22. Dishonor; infamy; disgraceful conduct
25. A morally wrong thing to do
27. Devout; religious
30. Although
31. Not conducive; harmful; adverse
35. Deep sorrow; grief; misfortune
36. Manner; way in which a person conducts himself
37. To become used to something disagreeable
38. She must wear a letter A
39. Place of worship
40. Jail

## DOWN
1. Worthy of reverence or respect
2. Annoys
3. Covering that darkens or obscures
4. Anticipated and disposed of effectively
5. Unfortunate; ill-omened
6. Cautious
8. Of a kind disposition; gentle or mild
10. Inventive skill or imagination; cleverness
11. A quality in something that arouses feelings of pity, sorrow, or sympathy
13. Make use of; benefit
17. Evil fame or reputation
18. Monarch; one who holds power over others
19. One's bearing or manner; appearance
21. Calmed; pacified
23. Expressed indirectly; hinted; suggested
24. Wise
26. To entreat; plead; beg
28. Compelled; urged to action by moral pressure
29. Lowered in rank; humbled; humiliated
32. To admit guilt
33. Sea transportation
34. Spirits; preachers try to save them
35. A woman who works for the devil

# VOCABULARY CROSSWORD ANSWER KEY - *The Scarlet Letter*

# VOCABULARY WORKSHEET 1 - *The Scarlet Letter*

Place the letter of the matching definition in the blank provided.

___ 1. Imperceptible          A. Make use of; benefit

___ 2. Sagacious              B. Wise

___ 3. Inauspicious           C. Unfortunate; ill-omened

___ 4. Err                    D. A compass of endeavor, influence or activity

___ 5. Venerable              E. Can't be explained

___ 6. Iniquity               F. Expressed indirectly; hinted; suggested

___ 7. Implied                G. Not able to be understood; mysterious

___ 8. Ingenuity              H. A quality in something that arouses feelings of pity, sorrow, or sympathy

___ 9. Avail                  I. Listed

___ 10. Pathos                J. Inventive skill or imagination; cleverness

___ 11. Intrusiveness         K. Not diminishing in speed, intensity or effort

___ 12. Ignominy              L. Not suitable; not agreeable

___ 13. Uncongenial           M. Sin; wickedness

___ 14. Inexplicable          N. Make a mistake

___ 15. Epoch                 O. Worthy of reverence or respect

___ 16. Unrelenting           P. Dishonor; infamy; disgraceful conduct

___ 17. Enumerated            Q. Milestone; particular point in time

___ 18. Orb                   R. Not capable of being discerned by the senses

___ 19. Impalpable            S. Not able to be touched

___ 20. Inscrutable           T. Coming in rudely or inappropriately; enter uninvited

# VOCABULARY WORKSHEET 2 - *The Scarlet Letter*

___ 1. Uncongenial          A. Milestone; particular point in time

___ 2. Inexplicable         B. To entreat; plead; beg

___ 3. Insurmountable       C. Compelled; urged to action by moral pressure

___ 4. Venerable            D. Evil fame or reputation

___ 5. Entreaties           E. Can't be explained

___ 6. Pathos               F. Something improper; incorrect; not appropriate

___ 7. Inevitable           G. Worthy of reverence or respect

___ 8. Err                  H. Make a mistake

___ 9. Epoch                I. Dishonor; infamy; disgraceful conduct

___ 10. Impelled            J. Coming between so as to hinder or modify

___ 11. Importunate         K. Pleas; petitions; requests

___ 12. Impute              L. To attribute

___ 13. Impropriety         M. Not suitable; not agreeable

___ 14. Implied             N. Not capable of being climbed or overcome

___ 15. Requite             O. Unreasonably persistent in a request or demand

___ 16. Intervening         P. Repay

___ 17. Implore             Q. Unavoidable

___ 18. Abased              R. A quality in something that arouses feelings of pity, sorrow, or sympathy

___ 19. Ignominy            S. Lowered in rank; humbled; humiliated

___ 20. Infamy              T. Expressed indirectly; hinted; suggested

# KEY: VOCABULARY WORKSHEETS - *The Scarlet Letter*

| Worksheet 1 | Worksheet 2 |
|---|---|
| 1. R | 1. M |
| 2. B | 2. E |
| 3. C | 3. N |
| 4. N | 4. G |
| 5. O | 5. K |
| 6. M | 6. R |
| 7. F | 7. Q |
| 8. J | 8. H |
| 9. A | 9. A |
| 10. H | 10. C |
| 11. T | 11. O |
| 12. P | 12. L |
| 13. L | 13. F |
| 14. E | 14. T |
| 15. Q | 15. P |
| 16. K | 16. J |
| 17. I | 17. B |
| 18. D | 18. S |
| 19. S | 19. I |
| 20. G | 20. D |

# VOCABULARY JUGGLE LETTER REVIEW GAME CLUES - *The Scarlet Letter*

| SCRAMBLED | WORD | CLUE |
|---|---|---|
| OARNDEME | DEMEANOR | Manner; way in which a person conducts himself |
| BAEDAS | ABASED | Lowered in rank; humbled; humiliated |
| TSHOAP | PATHOS | A quality in something that arouses feelings of pity, sorrow, or sympathy |
| LABEUIANM | UNAMIABLE | Not good-natured; not agreeable |
| LEEANBVRE | VENERABLE | Worthy of reverence or respect |
| EBAPILPMAL | IMPALPABLE | Not able to be touched |
| MEEDLIPL | IMPELLED | Compelled; urged to action by moral pressure |
| NNTGNRLIEUE | UNRELENTING | Not diminishing in speed, intensity or effort |
| LPAL | PALL | Covering that darkens or obscures |
| NEADUMEETR | ENUMERATED | Listed |
| IOUSP | PIOUS | Devout; religious |
| RRE | ERR | Make a mistake |
| RYWA | WARY | Cautious |
| ETOPTATEN | POTENTATE | Monarch; one who holds power or position over others |
| LIINIMCA | INIMICAL | Not conducive; harmful; adverse |
| PHCEO | EPOCH | Milestone; particular point in time |
| VTAODEIB | OBVIATED | Anticipated and disposed of effectively |
| GTEIUIYNN | INGENUITY | Inventive skill or imagination; cleverness |
| SICNAIUSUIOP | INAUSPICIOUS | Unfortunate; ill-omened |
| TYGNRICINOU | INCONGRUITY | Something that doesn't match with the facts or pattern |
| NIDERU | INURED | To become used to something disagreeable |
| ETNIENGVRIN | INTERVENING | Coming between so as to hinder or modify |
| EPTIUM | IMPUTE | To attribute |
| BOR | ORB | A compass of endeavor, influence or activity |
| RUPGNSUI | USURPING | Taking over |
| GSCSUOAIA | SAGACIOUS | Wise |
| IMNE | MIEN | One's bearing or manner; appearance |
| TELNBAIVEI | INEVITABLE | Unavoidable |
| FFQUA | QUAFF | Drink heartily |
| PRIOLEM | IMPLORE | To entreat; plead; beg |
| CAIDR | ACRID | Harsh; caustic; bitter |

| | | |
|---|---|---|
| VAALI | AVAIL | Make use of; benefit |
| GNENBI | BENIGN | Of a kind disposition; gentle |
| YUQIITIN | INIQUITY | Sin; wickedness |
| DEMIBU | IMBUED | Saturated; permeated |
| ELDPIIM | IMPLIED | Expressed indirectly; hinted; suggested |
| MEPPIIBECETRL | IMPERCEPTIBLE | Not capable of being discerned the senses |
| CTRUIYNDLIE | INCREDULITY | Disbelief |
| LAITEB | ALBEIT | Although |

www.ingramcontent.com/pod-product-compliance
Lightning Source LLC
Chambersburg PA
CBHW051417070526
44584CB00023B/3464